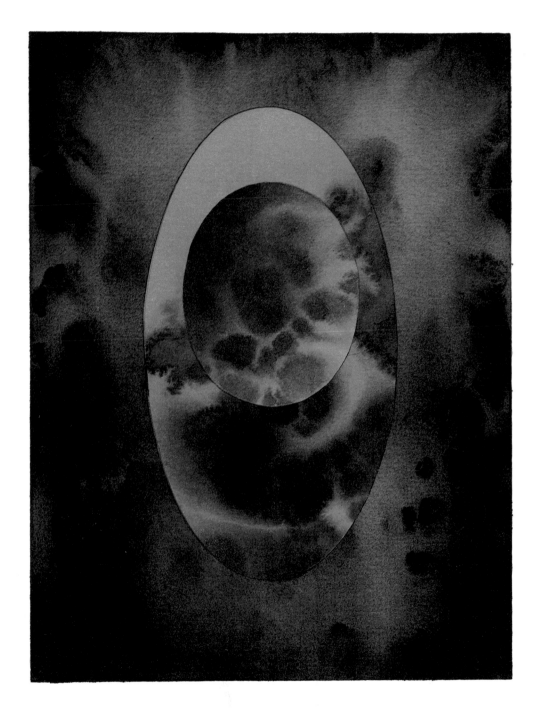

IN THE BEGINNING

Creation Stories from Around the World

Told by Virginia Hamilton

Illustrated by Barry Moser

HARCOURT BRACE JOVANOVICH, PUBLISHERS

San Diego · New York · London

Permission was granted to use primary source material
from: "Death and the Creator" in *The Origin of Life and
Death: African Creation Myths* by Ulli Beier, published by
Heineman Educational Books, Ltd.; *Tales Told in Togoland*
by A. W. Cardinall, published by Oxford University Press;
and "Australian Myth of the Great Father," in *Alpha* by
Charles A. Long, published by George Braziller, Inc. A list
of useful sources can be found on pages 159-161.

Library of Congress Cataloging-in-Publication Data
Hamilton, Virginia.
In the beginning: creation myths from around the world/told
by Virginia Hamilton; illustrated by Barry Moser.
p. cm.
Bibliography: p.
Summary: An illustrated collection of twenty-five myths from
various parts of the world explaining the creation of the world.
ISBN 0-15-238740-4
ISBN 0-15-238741-2 (ltd. edition)
1. Creation.   2. Mythology.   [1. Creation.   2. Mythology.
3. Folklore.]   I. Moser, Barry, ill.   II. Title.
BL226.H35 1988
291.2′4—dc19   88-6211
Printed in the United States of America
First edition
A B C D E

CONTENTS

A NOTE FROM THE AUTHOR

LET US think about when the earth was formed, or when the cosmos had nothing in it. Suppose there was a moment before time and space when the only things in existence were an object shaped like an egg and the darkness in which it was suspended. Suddenly, the egg cracks, and something slowly emerges from it. Imagine that the something from the egg is a great god who simply is *all there is*. That god makes the universe and humans and all things because that is the work of a god—to create.

Narratives in this book are stories called myths. They are about a god or gods, about superhuman beings, animals, plants, and about the first people on the earth. They are the truth to the people who believe in them and live by them. They give the people guidance and spiritual strength.

The narratives tell about events that caused astounding changes in the way humans feel, think, and act. The events described took place so long ago that it is almost impossible for us to imagine such a distant past.

Myth stories present themselves as truth and as accounts of

actual facts no matter how different these facts or truths may be from our ordinary, "real" experience. There are myths that are sacred or religious. And in all of them, there is the feeling that the unusual or divine events are inevitable.

We are more familiar with other forms of narratives similar to myths. Fairy tales, for example, also tell about extraordinary beings and happenings. But fairy tales take place *within* the time of human experience. They tell us stories that happened "once upon a time" in a recognizable past. They tell us about how things were then.

Myth stories about creation are different, however. In a prophetic voice, they relate events that seem outside of time and even beyond time itself. Creation myths take place before the "once upon a time" of fairy tales. They go *back beyond anything that ever was* and begin *before* anything has happened.

No attempt is made in a myth to prove the truth of its story to us. Its voice of authority relates an account of utter fact. Even the word *myth* comes from the Greek word *mythos* which means *word* in the sense of final authority.

The myths in this book tell us about acts of creation—the origin of the universe, god or gods, our world, a new beginning, and the creation of humankind.

The classic opening, although not the only opening, of a creation myth is "In the beginning. . . ." The most striking purpose of a creation myth is to explain something. Yet it also asks questions and gives reasons why groups of people perform certain rituals and live a particular way. Creation myths describe a place and a time impossible for us to see for ourselves. People everywhere have creation myths, revealing how they view themselves *to themselves* in ways that are movingly personal.

Creation, then, means the act of bringing into existence—something. The twenty-five creation myths in this book are about the origin of things. Limitations of space do not allow for all of the important world myths to be presented here. Also, not all myths are easily rendered on a level of understanding for many readers, while still keeping their authority in the language use and style of the original narratives.

These myths from around the world were created by people who sensed the wonder and glory of the universe. Lonely as they were, by themselves, early people looked inside themselves and expressed a longing to discover, to explain who they were, why they were, and from what and where they came.

Origin mythology identifies human beings as the highest of the animals and the lowest of the gods. It is where we fit. Our history as given in the myths shows our purpose. Along with all living things we must make the world a safe place for us to be ourselves.

In the Beginning shows us how humankind learned to live upon the earth. Let us read and enjoy these stories for their poetic beauty and the wondrous vision of the people who created them.

VIRGINIA HAMILTON

IN THE

BEGINNING

Raven and Man

THE PEA-POD MAN

Raven the Creator

Time was, there were no people on earth. The first man still lay inside the pea pod.

Four days passed, and on the fifth day, he pushed with his feet. He broke through the bottom of the pod and fell to the ground. When he got up, he had become a grown man. He looked at everything and himself, his arms and legs, his hands; felt his neck. The pod that had held him still hung on the vine with a hole in its bottom.

The grown man walked a little away from the pod where he had started. The ground under him felt as if it were moving, too. It was not firm, but soft.

The way it moved under him made him feel sick. He stood still, and slowly a pool of water formed at his feet. He bent down and drank from the pool. It felt good the way the water went from his mouth down inside of him. It made him feel better.

He stood up again, refreshed. Next, he saw something. It was a dark thing flapping along, and it was coming. Then, it was there before him. It stood looking at him.

It was Raven. Raven lifted one of his wings and pushed his beak up to his forehead. He raised it like a mask. And when he moved his beak up, Raven changed into a man. He walked all around the first man to get a good look at him.

"Who are you?" Raven asked, at last. "Where did you come from?"

"I came from the pea pod," said the man, pointing to the vine and the broken pod.

"I made that vine!" said Raven. "I never thought something like you would come from it. Here, this ground we're standing on is soft. I made it later than the rest. Let's go to the high ground. It's hard and thick."

Man and Raven went to the high ground, and it was quite hard under them.

"Did you have anything to eat?" Raven asked.

Man told him about the wet stuff that had pooled at his feet.

"Ah, you must have drunk water," Raven said. "Wait here for me."

He drew the beak-mask down and changed once more into a bird. Raven flew up into the sky and disappeared.

Four days later, he returned. The whole time, Man had been waiting.

Raven pushed up his beak and was again a man. He had four berries—two raspberries and two heathberries.

"I made these for you," he said. "I want them to grow all over the earth. Here, eat them."

Man put the berries in his mouth and ate them.

"I feel better," he said.

Next, Raven took Man to a small creek. There, the man-bird found two pieces of clay and molded them into tiny mountain sheep. He held them on his palm. When they dried, he let Man take a close look at them.

"They look nice," Man said.

"Now shut your eyes," Raven told him. Man did close his eyes.

Raven pulled down his beak and made his wings wave back and forth, back and forth over the clay figures. They came to life and bounded away as grown mountain sheep. Raven lifted his mask.

"Look!" he said.

Man saw the sheep moving very fast. They were full of life, and that pleased him. He thought people would like them. For there were more men growing on the vine.

But when Raven saw the way Man was looking at the mountain sheep with such delight, he put them up high so that people would not kill too many of them.

Raven made more animals, moved his wings, and brought them to life. Every animal and bird and fish that Raven made, Man viewed with pleasure. That worried Raven. He thought he'd better create something Man would fear, or else Man might eat or kill everything that moved.

So Raven went to another creek. He took some clay and created a bear, making it come alive. Quickly, Raven got out of

Woman

the way of Bear because the animal was so fierce it would tear him apart and maybe eat him.

"You will get lonely if you stay by yourself," Raven said to Man. "So I will make somebody for you."

Raven went off a ways, where he could view Man but where Man couldn't be sure what he was doing. There, off a ways, he made a figure out of clay much like Man's, although different. He fastened watercress on the back of its head for hair. When the figure had dried in the palm of his hand, he waved his wings several times. It came to life. It was a lovely woman. She got up, grew up, and stood beside Man.

"That is your helper and your mate," said Raven.

"She is very pretty," said Man, and he was happy.

Raven went on doing what he needed to do. And Man and Woman had a child. Soon, there were many, many people and animals. All that was living grew and thrived.

The world prospered.

COMMENT: *This is a wonderful, dramatic Eskimo myth, parts of which are widely known, spread from Siberia to Greenland. The myth speaks of society rather than the universe. Raven is a trickster god who travels from heaven to earth and sometimes, in some stories, to the seafloor. He has sacred power and can change form. Raven instructs people in living. He creates first-man through the pea vine and other people and animals from clay taken from the earth-creek.*

Quatgoro

FINDING NIGHT

Quat the Creator

In the beginning, there was light. It never dimmed, this light over everything. It was bright all-light everywhere, and there was no rest from it.

Under the light was a huge stone. The stone was the mother, Quatgoro. Quatgoro split in half, and there came twelve sons born into the light. They were Quat and his eleven brothers.

The brothers were all named Tangaro, but they were not the same. The first brother after Quat was Tangaro the Wise. The second was Tangaro the Fool. The names of the other nine were names of leaves, such as Breadfruit Leaf, Coconut Leaf, Bamboo Leaf, and so on. They all grew up as soon as they were born, just as Quat had.

Quat named himself when he was born. He had no father to name him. Right away, he thought about making men. And he thought about making other things—plants, pigs, and stones.

Quat made the first human from a tree. He carved arms and then legs, and he made the rest of the body apart from them. He made fingers and hands, toes and feet. He made ears and eyes—all neatly and carefully. Then he fitted the parts together.

He made six of these wood puppets. And he stood them in a line so he could do a sacred dance in front of them.

Soon the puppets began to move. They moved just a little at first; they moved stiffly. But they moved. Quat beat on his sacred drum. The drumbeats were like magic. The puppets moved more with each beat. They moved faster until they were doing the dance of life to the drumbeats.

Now the puppets that had life were able to stand, to walk, to run along. Quat fixed them into men and women. There were three women and three men. Each of the women had a husband, and each of the men had a wife. That is the way it was.

Quat was being watched by his brother, who was Tangaro the Fool. Everything the Fool did came out wrong. But he thought he would make men and women, too, as Quat had.

"Think I'll cut down a tree," he thought. And he did, but it was different from Quat's tree. Still, Tangaro the Fool carved six model puppets as he had seen Quat do. He propped them up and did a dance in front of them. He beat the drum to give his puppets life. He saw them move. But he dug a pit and buried them, he was so stupid. Then he left them and went away.

A week later, Tangaro the Fool remembered the six figures he had made from the tree wood. He had forgotten all about them. He dug up the earth where they were, and he scraped it from them.

What he found there had rotted. He was forced to leave his puppets buried, they smelled so bad. So this, then, was the beginning of Death. That is the way Death came to the world, when Tangaro the Fool buried his wood figures and they rotted.

Meanwhile, brother Quat was making pigs. At first he had them stand up on two legs and walk that way. When his brothers saw this, they pointed and laughed and laughed.

"Your pigs look like men!" they exclaimed.

Quat didn't want the pigs to be laughed at. So he shortened their front legs. Now the pigs walked on four feet instead of two. They walk that way even now.

In this way Quat made many things. He thought to make all kinds of plants, canoes—all kinds of things.

"It's too light," his brothers said one day. "Quat, do something. We don't like the world so bright all of the time. Make something to stop it, please, Quat."

Quat looked everywhere for something. Something that was not light. He could find nothing. Light was everywhere. But he thought about making a place without light. He'd heard about such a place at the far edge of the sky, and it was called *Qong*, Night. Quat tied a pig to his canoe and sailed over the sea toward the far edge.

He sailed and sailed. Finally, Quat reached the edge where the sky came down and he could touch it. There lived Qong.

Night was dark. It had no light anywhere in it. It touched

Quat about his eyes and gave him the blackest eyebrows. It taught him sleep, as well. And the great darkness, Night, gave him another piece of itself.

So Quat went home, taking the piece of Night in his hand. On the way, he stopped at the Torres Islands. He gave the people his pig and a small bit of his piece of Night. They gave him birds of all kinds. That is why the Torres have pigs and night to this day.

When Quat reached home, he brought darkness with him. And he brought birds which always follow the night with their noise of waking. That is how we tell that day is coming.

Quat's brothers were waiting for him.

"Hurry," said Quat. "I will show you how to make your beds."

He showed them how to use coco fronds, which he spread on the floor. Then he showed his brothers how to lie down and how to rest, ready for sleep.

"Look, the sun is going," said the brothers. "Will it return again?"

"Night is getting ready," Quat said. And he let the piece of Night come from his hand.

"What is this that covers everything and the sky?" his brothers asked.

"It is Night," said Quat. "Lie down; be still."

The brothers did lie down, and they soon felt weightless and dreamlike. Not long after, their eyes closed.

"I think we must be dying," said the brothers.

"It is just sleep," said Quat. "That's what it is called."

The birds knew about Night and how long it would be. They could tell; they could feel it passing by. As it passed, they chirped, whistled, and squawked.

Quat took a sharp, red stone and cut a hole in Night. The first light that came out of the tear was red light. And then all of the light shone brightly. The birds made noise, for they knew what first light looked like.

The brothers' eyes opened wide; they started their chores.

This is the way it is for us: Night comes. We sleep. Birds cry.

We wake. Day comes. We work. All because of Quat.

Day in, day out.

COMMENT: *Quat is the solar god of the Banks Islands, north of the New Hebrides in Melanesia. The tales about him are many and varied. This myth relates a beginning filled with light. Rather than creating light, Quat must discover Night. There are twelve sons of Quatgoro, the great seed, one for each month of the year. If Quat's foolish brother hadn't buried his wood puppets, humankind would have lived forever. But because of the brother's stupidity, Death was brought into the world. Yet Quat travels to the edge of the horizon, or the end of creation, where he finds the night, brings it back, and is able to finish his own making of the world.*

Sa

AN ENDLESS SEA OF MUD

Death the Creator

In the beginning there was darkness. And in it lived Death, called Sa, with his wife and daughter. The three of them were all that was.

There was nowhere for them to live comfortably, so Sa started it. He used his magic power, and he made an endless mud sea. In this mud place, Sa built his house.

After that, the God Ala-tan-gana came to visit Sa. He found Sa's house dirty and dark. Alatangana thought Sa should do better than that, and he said so.

"Nothing can live in such a place," the God told Sa. "This house needs fixing up. Everything is too dark."

So Alatangana thought he'd better take things in hand. He made the mud solid. We know it now as Earth. "The earth feels sad," God said. "I will make plants and animals to live on it." So he did.

Now this work of God Alatangana made Sa very happy. He felt quite friendly toward the God for all of his help, and he welcomed him into his house.

It was not long before Alatangana asked Sa for the hand of his daughter in marriage.

Sa made excuses, for he was fond of his daughter and did not want to lose her just yet. And finally, Sa had to say no. But by this time, Alatangana had talked with the young woman. They came to their own understanding. They married in secret. And then they ran off to get away from Sa's anger.

They escaped to a far corner of the new earth. There they were quite content. It was not long before they had a house full of children. There were seven girls and seven boys. There were three boys and three girls who were black. And there were four boys and four girls who were white. Thus, there were six black children and eight white children that were all the sons and daughters of the God Alatangana and Sa's only child.

A strange thing happened. These children spoke different languages. Their parents could not understand them. The God Alatangana didn't know what to make of it. Finally, he went off to ask Sa to help him.

When the God reached Sa's home, he was not greeted warmly.

"I punished you," Sa said, "because you stole my daughter. Now and forever, you will not understand what your children say. Your white children shall use ink and pen to write down what they think. Your black children shall know how to feed themselves. I will give them useful tools to work with—the axe, and the hoe, and the machete.

"I tell you," Sa went on, "have the white children marry only their own color, their own kind. And have the black children marry their own kind."

Alatangana didn't like this at all, but he wanted no more trouble with Sa. At last, he agreed to Sa's command.

The God went home and praised all of his children. And when the children grew and married, they set out for the four corners of the earth. That is why there are black people and white people everywhere over the earth.

So it is that from the children of Alatangana and Death's daughter came all of the earth's children. We know them by the names of the countries where they live. There are German children, and Kono children, and on, and on—so many names!

Yet the world was still dark, and the people lived in the dark.

"I know," said the God. "I'll send the tou-tou bird and the rooster to ask Sa what to do."

And he did.

The two messengers went to Sa. Sa said to them, "Here is a song for each of you. I give it to you to call forth the light of day. Then humans can see to go about their work."

The rooster and the tou-tou went back home to the God. First the tou-tou bird sang, and then the cock. Right away there was the first day coming. It dawned.

Behold! The sun!

The sun moved across the sky. At the end of its journey, it found a place to sleep on the other side of the earth.

Next came the stars to give just enough light for people to get around in the dark. Then Sa brought the moon to comfort people.

Sa called the God to his home. Alatangana went there. Sa told him, "I welcomed you into my home, and you repaid me by taking my daughter. Now you must give me one of your children on the earth whenever I call one to me. The child will hear a rattling calabash gourd in its dreams. Then it will know I have called it. The call of Sa must be answered!"

It is true. The God Alatangana stole Death's daughter. He never paid the bride-price. Now and forever, human beings must die when Sa calls them. When they hear the calabash rattle, the sound will be Death calling.

Still, there is some good that came out of bad. Now and forever, two birds sing forth the day. First the tou-tou, then the cock.

COMMENT: *In this creation myth from the Kono people of Guinea, Death lives in darkness before we know of the God Alatangana. The meaning is clear that Death came first, made mud, and then the God came to make solid earth out of the mud. The myth is also an explanation of how various races came to live all over the world, and why the races would seem to be separate from one another. It also tells how the sun, moon, and stars came to be.*

The God Alatangana has less power than Sa, Death. And because of the God's wrongdoing, Death is brought into the lives of humans. The God stole Sa's only daughter. Ever after, when it pleases him, Death takes one of God's children.

The Cosmic Egg

BURSTING FROM THE HEN'S EGG

Phan Ku the Creator

The space of the universe was in the shape of a hen's egg. Within the egg was a great mass called *no thing*. Inside *no thing* was something not yet born. It was not yet developed, and it was called Phan Ku.

In no time, Phan Ku burst from the egg. He was the first being. He was the Great Creator. Phan Ku was the size of a giant. He grew ten feet a day and lived for eighteen thousand years.

Hair grew all over Phan Ku. Horns curved up out of his head, and tusks jutted from his jaw. In one hand he held a chisel; and with it he carved out the world.

Phan Ku separated sky from earth. The light, pure sky was *yang*, and the heavy, dark weight of earth was *yin*. The vast Phan Ku himself filled the space between earth and sky, yin and yang.

He chiseled out earth's rivers; he scooped out the valleys. It was easy for him to layer the mountains and pile them high upon high.

Then Phan Ku placed the stars and moon in the night sky

Phan Ku

and the sun into the day. He put the great seas where they are now, and he showed the people how to fashion ships, how to build bridges.

Only when Phan Ku died was the world at last complete. The dome of the sky was made from Phan Ku's skull. Soil was formed from his body. Rocks were made from his bones; rivers and seas, from his blood. All of plant life came from Phan Ku's hair. Thunder and lightning are the sound of his voice. The wind and the clouds are his breath. Rain was made from his sweat. And from the fleas that lived in the hair covering him came all of humankind.

The form of Phan Ku vanished in the making of the world. After he was gone, there was room then for pain, and that is how suffering came to human beings.

COMMENT: *This cosmic egg type myth from China dates from 600 B.C. Phan Ku was a popular god of the period, and there are many variations of this legend. He completes the creation of the world by means of his own sacrifice. The sky dome comes from his skull, and his body's vermin becomes humanity. Because the god was sacred, humanity was sacred. But by losing the living god Phan Ku, humanity loses its creator and therefore suffers forever.*

Old Man

TRAVELING TO FORM THE WORLD

Old Man the Creator

He was out there, traveling all over and making things. Old Man. He had been south and was on his way north. He created the birds and animals as he went. He made prairies, always traveling north, and mountains.

They say that first he made timber and brushlands. He put red paint in the soil, and he formed rivers and waterfalls. He was making the world that stands here today. He formed the river called Milk, the Teton. Then he went across it.

He was getting tired. So he climbed a hill, and he lay down to take a rest.

Old Man stretched out on his back on the hill. He lay his arms straight out from his shoulders. He had stones to outline himself, marking him from his head to his feet. Those stones are right there where they marked him, even today.

After a good rest, Old Man again headed on to the north. He stumbled once and fell. There was a knoll there; it brought him to his knees when he tripped.

"You are something bad to be stumbling on," said Old Man.

He raised two buttes there, large ones. And he named them the Knees, which they are still called today.

He went on. And he carried more rocks. These he used to make the Sweet Grass Hills of Montana.

Old Man decided one day that he would make a mother and her child. He formed them out of clay. He molded the clay in the shape of humans. And he spoke to them.

"You will be people," he said. He covered up the clay shapes and went away.

Next morning, Old Man went to the place, taking the covering off the shapes. They seemed to have changed just a little. The morning after that, the shapes had changed some more. And the next day, they were different still.

On the fourth morning, Old Man went over and looked at the shapes that were images of people now.

"Rise up. Walk," Old Man told them. And they rose up and started walking. They, the woman and child and their maker, walked to the river.

"My name is Na'pi," he told them, which means Old Man.

The woman looked at the water and said to Old Man, "Tell me, how will it be? Will we live always? Will there be no end to our living?"

"Well, I haven't ever thought about it," Old Man said. "We'll have to decide. Let me take this buffalo chip and throw it in the river. If it floats, then people will die. But they will die for only four days. Four days after they die, they will live once again."

Then, Old Man said this: "If the buffalo chip sinks, then there will be an end to people's lives."

He threw the chip in the water. It floated.

The woman bent down and picked up a stone.

"No," she said. "Let me throw this stone in the river. If it floats, we will live forever. But if it sinks, we will feel sorry for one another, that we must all die."

The woman threw the stone in the water. It sank.

"So, you have chosen," said Old Man. "There will be an end to people."

COMMENT: *"Old Man" is an origin story, a folk myth of the Blackfoot American Indian people. The creator, Old Man, comes from the south and is on his way around as the story begins. It is as if he walks down through the ages, shaping and making his creations as he goes. The earth is not quite formed or finished. And Old Man finds there is much for him to do to make it ready for people. In this story, woman is the spoiler. She throws a stone, which sinks. Thus, people will die and feel sorrow and pity for one another.*

Erlik's Face in the Mud

FIRST MAN BECOMES THE DEVIL

Ulgen the Creator

God Ulgen saw mud floating on the waters. The mud had the shape of a human face. Ulgen gave the shape a spirit, and when it lived, it was the first man. Ulgen called him Erlik.

In the beginning, Erlik and God Ulgen were friends. But then Erlik tried to create life of his own. He boasted about it.

"I can do as well as Ulgen. I can make a man."

That made Ulgen angry. He commanded Erlik down to the depths. Now Erlik is the leader of dead spirits. He is the devil. Sometimes Erlik comes forth, and Ulgen must command him down again.

Ulgen next created earth.

He put seven trees on it, and he put a man under each of the seven trees.

Ulgen made a golden mountain, and there he also placed a tree, which was the eighth one.

Under this tree he put the eighth man.

Ulgen named that eighth man Maidere.

Then Ulgen, the god, went away.

Each of the seven trees grew seven branches after seven years. There was one branch for each year. But each man under each tree did not change at all. Each man stayed the same.

Ulgen returned.

"Why do the men not change?" he asked the eighth man, Maidere.

"Well, they cannot grow and change when there are no women for them," Maidere said.

"Then come down from your golden mountain," said Ulgen. "Make women for these men."

And Ulgen walked away again.

Maidere came down. He started to create a woman. He created her body, but he could not find a way to make this first woman live.

He had to find Ulgen. And he left Dog to guard his creation.

"If anyone comes, bare your teeth," Maidere told Dog. "Bark very loud, and frighten him away. Don't let anyone come near the woman."

"All right, just as you say," Dog said.

Maidere was barely away when the devil Erlik came along.

"Dog," Erlik said, "would you like a fur coat?"

In those days, Dog had nothing on his skin. He was naked Dog. It was winter and cold. And he was shivering Dog.

"The coat I give you will never wear out," Erlik said. "It will feel cool in summer and warm in winter. And you know that any fur coat I give you will last you all your life."

"So what do you want me to do in return?" asked trembling Dog.

"Just let me look at the woman Maidere has made. I only want to see her."

"Well, all right," Dog said. "As you wish."

Erlik crept close to the woman.

He took out his flute and played seven tones into the woman's nose. Next he played an instrument with nine strings right in her ear.

The woman sat up. All at once, she was quite alive. She had a mind, and she had a spirit. But she had seven tempers and nine moods.

Dog found this out when the woman got angry for no reason and threw stones at him.

When Maidere came back home, he carried the breath of life from God Ulgen.

But he was too late.

This first woman didn't need the breath of life. She was already alive.

"I told you not to let anybody near the woman!" Maidere scolded Dog.

"Well, I was cold," Dog said. "Erlik said he would give me a fur coat."

Warm Dog

"In that case, I will have the fur coat grow on your back forever," Maidere said. "Let everybody throw stones at you forever and treat you badly forever, too."

"All right," sighed warm Dog.

So it has always been.

COMMENT: *There are many versions of this Russian Altaic creation story in which first man is the devil, Erlik. In other stories, God Ulgen is first man and is himself created.*

In this story, the eighth man, Maidere, must bring the breath of life from God to the first woman. The story ends as a pour quoi *or why* tale—explaining why the dog has fur, and why the woman has a bad temper.

In a Siberian Tatar version, the god Pajana must go to heaven and receive life for his creations from the High God. Although he leaves the naked dog to guard over them, Erlik comes and spits on them. When Pajana returns with life, he finds he must turn his creations inside out in order to cleanse them of the devil's work.

The Rope of Feathers

TURTLE DIVES TO THE BOTTOM OF THE SEA

Earth Starter the Creator

In the beginning, all was dark. There was water everywhere. There was no sun and no moon and no stars.

Then a raft came from the north, floating on the water. There were just two in the raft. They were Turtle and Pehe-ipe.

Down from the sky came a rope of feathers. And down the rope came Earth Starter. When he was all the way down, he tied the rope to the raft and then climbed into it.

Earth Starter's face was covered, and so it could not be seen. His body was shining as if the sun shone on it. He sat down and said not a word until he was spoken to.

"Where do you come from?" Turtle asked.

"I come from above," Earth Starter said.

"Make me some dry land, Brother," said Turtle. "Can you do that? Sometimes I would like to come up out of the water."

When Earth Starter didn't answer, Turtle asked, "Will there be people in this world?"

Earth Starter thought about that. Finally, he said, "Yes."

"How long will it be before you make some people?" Turtle wanted to know.

"I don't know," said Earth Starter. "You want dry land, but how am I going to get some earth to make the dry land?"

"Well, tie a rope around my leg," Turtle said. "I'll dive down underwater for some earth."

So Earth Starter did what Turtle said. He took the other end of the rope down from above, and he tied it to Turtle.

"If the rope is not long enough to reach all the way," said Turtle, "I will jerk the rope once. Then you must pull me up. But if it is long enough, I'll give two jerks on it. Then you must pull me up fast, and I will have all the earth I can hold."

As Turtle went over the side of the boat, Pehe-ipe began to shout.

Turtle was gone six years. When he finally came up, he was covered with green slime. The only earth he had was the tiny bit under his nails. The rest had melted away in the water.

Earth Starter took a knife and scraped the earth from Turtle's nails. He placed the earth in his own palm and rolled it until it was round. It was about as round as a small pebble. And, carefully, he placed the earth pebble on the back of the raft.

Earth Starter kept going over to look at the pebble. Two times he went, and it hadn't done anything. The third time, the earth pebble had grown as big around as his arms. The fourth time he went over, it was as large as the whole world.

The raft got stuck on dry land. So now there was land, but Turtle wasn't yet satisfied. "It's dark all the time. I can't stay here. Can't you make light? I want to see."

Earth Starter said, "We will get out of the raft, first. Then we'll see what can be done."

The three of them got out—Turtle, Pehe-ipe, and Earth Starter.

"Look that way, to the east," said Earth Starter. "I'll tell my sister to come up."

A light began to grow. It was daybreak. Pehe-ipe shouted. The Sun came up.

"Which way will the Sun travel?" asked Turtle.

"I'll tell her to come this way," said Earth Starter. "And I'll tell her to go down over there."

When the Sun did go down, Pehe-ipe started to cry and shout. It grew quite dark out.

"So how do you like everything?" Earth Starter asked the other two.

"It's just fine," Turtle said. "But is this all you're going to do for us?"

"I'm going to do more," said Earth Starter.

He called to the stars, and they came out. Next, he made a great oak tree grow. The three of them sat in its shade for two days.

After two days, they all went off to look at the world that Earth Starter had made. They began just when the Sun came up. And they were back by the time she was going down. Earth Starter went so fast that the other two saw him as a ball of fire flashing underground and underwater.

While they were looking at the world, Coyote and his dog, Rattlesnake, came up from the ground. Coyote could see Earth Starter's face, but neither he nor anyone else were allowed to go inside Earth Starter's house.

When he was back, Earth Starter called the birds into the air. He made all of the trees. He took mud and made the first deer. Then he made all of the animals.

Turtle said more than once about the animals, "That one doesn't look good. Make it some other way."

After that, Earth Starter told Coyote something.

"I will make people," Earth Starter said, and he did.

He took the red earth and mixed it with water. He made a man and a woman. He laid the man down on his right side and the woman on his left side. They were inside his house. Earth Starter lay down flat on his back with his arms outstretched. He lay that way and sweated all day and night.

The next morning, early, the woman began to tickle him in the side. He stayed still. He never laughed. The man and the woman were very white. Their eyes were pink. Their hair was black, and their teeth were so bright.

Earth Starter didn't finish their hands. He didn't know the best way to do it.

Well, Coyote saw the man and woman. He said they ought to have hands like he had. Paws. But Earth Starter said no.

"Their hands shall be like mine," Earth Starter said.

"Why is that?" Coyote wanted to know.

The First Deer

"So when they are chased by bears," said Earth Starter, "they can climb trees."

The first man was named Ku'ksu. The first woman was called Morning-star Woman.

Coyote asked, so Earth Starter told him how he'd made the people.

"That's not hard," thought Coyote. "I can do that myself." He did it the way Earth Starter told him.

But early in the morning when the woman poked him in the side, he couldn't help laughing. Because Coyote couldn't stay still and quiet, the woman would not come to life.

"I told you not to laugh, Coyote," Earth Starter said.

"I didn't laugh," Coyote said.

That was the first lie.

Time passed, and there were many people. Earth Starter wanted it easy for them. He didn't want them to have to work. He made the fruits easy to find. And no one was ever to be sick or to die.

As more and more people came, Earth Starter did not come as often. In the night, he would come to see Ku'ksu, the first man.

One night, he said to Ku'ksu, "In the morning, go to the lake near here. Take the people with you. I will make you an old man before you get there."

And by the time Ku'ksu got to the lake, he was an old, old man. He fell into the lake, sinking way under, out of sight.

The ground began to shake, and waves overflowed the lake shore. There was a roaring like thunder.

Then Ku'ksu came back up from underwater. He was a young man again.

Earth Starter said to the people, "Do as I say, and everything will be well. When you grow so old you can no longer walk quickly, come here to this lake. If you have to, get someone to bring you. Then you must go down under the water just as Ku'ksu did. And you will come up young again."

After he spoke, Earth Starter went away in the night.

He went up above.

COMMENT: *This origin myth from the Maidu Indians of California is an* Earth-Diver *type, in which a creature dives into water, or back to nature. By plunging into water, the old is washed away, and the new creation may begin. The power of the god, Earth Starter, is clear. He creates Ku'ksu, man, and allows him to be reborn in the way the world begins—by going underwater and coming up young again. Perhaps the first people were too frightened to follow the first man into the lake and so do not live forever as he does.*

Creation myths do not always give reasons for the way people are or the manner in which things happen. We don't know Pehe-ipe's importance in this story, for example, or why he shouts and cries. He simply does at certain times, and we accept that he does without explanation.

Nana Buluku

MOON AND SUN

Mawu-Lisa the Creators

Nana Buluku, the Great Mother, created the world. She had twins, Mawu and Lisa. She did nothing after that.

Mawu was the moon who had power over the night and lived in the west. Lisa was the sun, who made his home in the east. At first, Mawu and Lisa had no offspring. But then, when there was an eclipse—when one of them was in the shadow of the other or another heavenly body—they came together and created children.

Mawu and Lisa were Mother and Father of all the other gods. And there were fourteen of these gods, who were seven pairs of twins. The gods of earth, storm, and iron were born first.

One day, Mawu-Lisa called all of their children to come around them. When they all came, Mawu-Lisa gave each pair of twins a good place to rule. The first twins were told to rule earth.

"Take what you wish from our heaven," Mawu-Lisa told them.

The second pair of twins were told to stay in the sky.

Thunder and Lightning

"You will rule over thunder and lightning," said Mawu-Lisa.

The third pair, who were iron, were the strength of their parents.

"You will clear the forests and prepare the land," Mawu-Lisa said. "And you will give humans their tools and weapons."

The next twins were to live in the sea.

"Children, rule all waters and all fishes," Mawu-Lisa commanded.

Other twins would rule over the birds and beasts of the bush country. They would take care of all of the trees everywhere.

More twins were to take care of the space between the earth and sky. "And you will also make the length of time that humans shall live," said Mawu-Lisa.

Then Mawu said, "Come visit me. You will tell me everything that goes on in the world."

Mawu-Lisa took care that none of the lesser gods were ever seen by human beings. That is why people speak so of the sky as a spirit, and speak of storms and lightning as spirits, too. And all of it is because of the power of the sky gods, Moon and Sun, Mawu-Lisa.

COMMENT: *This is a myth of the Fon people of Abomey (Republic of Benin). The Fon were the first inhabitants of Dahomey in the twelfth century. The myth is one of many stories of Mawu and Lisa, who were partners in the sky and often said to be twins.*

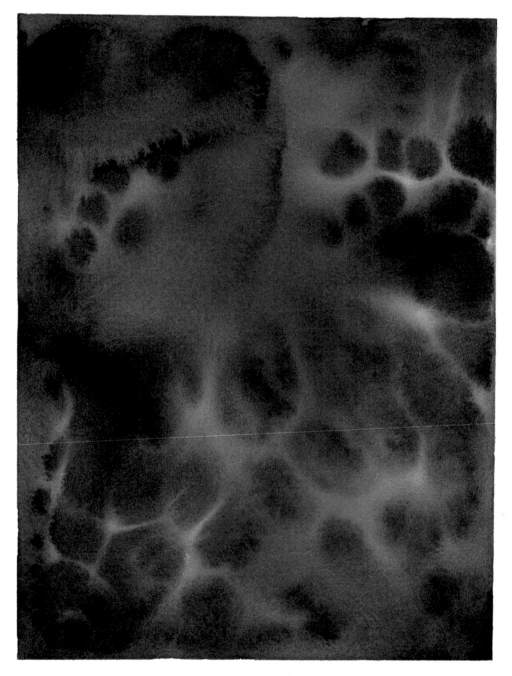

The Great Tangle of Night

BANDICOOTS COME FROM HIS BODY

Karora the Creator

In the beginning, all was darkness forever. Night covered the earth in a great tangle.

Ka-ro-ra lay asleep at the very bottom of the deep, dry ground of Il-ba-lint-ja. Covering Karora like a shell was the soil. It was red with flowers and overflowing with grasses of many kinds.

A great, decorated pole sprang from the midst of the grasses atop the ground of Ilbalintja. The pole rose up and up towards the sky, reaching up to the heavens. It swayed above Karora; his head lay at the root of it where he had rested from the very beginning.

Karora was thinking: wishes and dreams flashed through his mind. Bandicoots, those large rats, started coming out of his navel and from his armpits. And they leaped up out of the ground and burst into life.

The dawn appeared. The sun rose at Ilbalintja and flooded everything with light.

Karora, the bandicoot ancestor, got up now that the sun had come. He burst through the earth crust that had covered him, leaving a gaping hole where he had been. The hole became the Ilbalintja Soak. And now it was filled with the sweet dark juice of honeysuckle buds. Karora was hungry, since the magical powers had gone out of him.

His eyes fluttered, and he could open them just a little. He groped about and felt a squirming mass of bandicoots. He stood more firmly on his feet.

Karora was thinking that he wanted something to eat. He took hold of two young bandicoots. Cooked them close to the spot where the sun stood in the white-hot ground. The sun heated the food with its fiery fingers.

After he'd eaten, the bandicoot ancestor thought about having somebody to help him. But the sun was going down now. It covered itself with necklaces made from hair and string. Then it disappeared from sight.

Karora fell asleep with his arms outstretched on each side.

Something in the shape of a bull-roarer[1] came from under his armpit.

The bull-roarer took on human form. In one night, it grew into a young man. He was Karora's firstborn son. Karora woke up feeling something heavy on his arm. It was his son resting on his shoulder. But the son had no life yet.

---

[1]A piece of flat wood pointed at both ends with a hole in one where a hair string is threaded. Bull-roarers are twirled around and around in ceremonies. Young men come quickly when they hear their humming, whistling sound.

Morning came, and Karora got up. He was adorned with ceremonial designs worked in blood from his skin and bird-feather down. Then the bandicoot ancestor sounded the loud, vibrating call that all knew as rai-an-kintja. That was how the son was stirred to life. The son got up and danced the ceremonial dance around his father, Karora.

The first ceremony came to an end. Karora had his son kill the bandicoots playing nearby in the shade. The young man got them, and the father cooked them in the white-hot soil. He shared the cooked meat with his son.

Evening came, and both father and son went to sleep. Two more sons were born that night to the father, from his armpits. The next morning, Karora called them to life, using the loud call as before. For many days and nights, the borning went on. The sons hunted. The father brought more and more sons to life. Sometimes there were as many as fifty born in a single night.

Finally the bandicoot ancestor and his sons had eaten all of the bandicoots that had sprung from his body. He had to send out his many sons to search the great Ilbalintja Plain for food. They searched for hours in the tall white grass. But all was empty of bandicoots.

For three days they hunted, only to return hungry and tired each time.

All at once, they heard a sound like a whirling bull-roarer. They listened. They thought it might be a man swinging the bull-roarer. They hunted him and searched, hitting the bandicoot nests and stabbing with their sticks.

Something dark and hairy scurried away. Someone shouted, "There goes a sandhill wallaby!" The sons hurled their sticks after the kangaroo. A stick hit it and broke its leg. The injured wallaby started to sing:

"I, T-jen-ter-ama, have now grown lame. The purple ever-lastings[2] are clinging to me. I am a man as you are. I am not a bandicoot."

With that, the lame Tjenterama limped away.

The brothers went on their way home. Soon they saw their father coming toward them. Karora led them back to the soak. All of the young men sat down on its edge in circles, like the water's widening ripples. And a vast flood of sweet honey from the honeysuckle buds covered them. It swirled them back into the Ilbalintja Soak.

Karora of the ages stayed where he was. The sons were carried by the flood underground three miles farther on. There they joined Tjenterama, whose leg had been broken by one of their sticks.

Here now is what the people of the Bandicoot Clan do and say today. On the new ceremonial ground, they point out the rocks and stones that stand for the undying bodies of Karora's sons. These lie on top of a round stone that is said to be Tjenter-ama's body. Tjenterama, who the sons had injured in the past, is the new chief. In all of the bandicoot ceremonies of today, Tjen-terama is said to be the chief of Ilbalintja.

[2]daisies

Karora, so the people say, stayed in his first home. He lies forever asleep at the bottom of the Ilbalintja Soak. And those who come to the soak to quench their thirst can do so only if they bring bunches of green boughs. These they must place at the edge of the soak.

Then, Karora, the great bandicoot ancestor, is so happy
that they have come. He smiles in his sleep.

COMMENT: *The dreamlike "Karora" myth is from the Australian Northern Aranda aborigines of the Bandicoot Totem. It is an example of the* Imperfect Creation *type of origin myth. There are not enough bandicoots for a stable food supply for all of the sons created. The world is destroyed in a flood of honey.*

In western biblical history, imperfect humans are destroyed when it rains forty days and forty nights, which causes a flood. In this type of myth, what is created by a god must be made perfect, or it is destroyed.

His Blue Heavenly Self

SPIDER ANANSE FINDS *SOMETHING*

Wulbari the Creator

In the beginning, God was Wul-bar-i. And God Wulbari was heaven—spread not five feet above the mother, earth.

The God was very upset. There was not enough space between Him and earth. The man who lived on earth kept bumping his head against the God. It didn't seem to bother the man, but it surely bothered Wulbari.

An old woman was making food outside her hut. Her stirring pole kept knocking and poking Wulbari. The smoke from her cooking fires got into his eyes.

"I'll rise up a bit," thought Wulbari.

And so He lifted the blue of his heavenly self just a little higher.

"There," He thought, "that's better."

But still, being so close to women and men, Wulbari was useful. He became a perfect towel for everybody. And the people used Him to wipe their dirty hands. There was even one woman who took a piece of clean blue to make her soup taste better.

"Ummmm," she murmured.

Wulbari couldn't believe it. But there it was, pieces of Heaven-He being sniffed by the dogs and eaten by babies.

Wulbari moved up higher and higher until He was out of the way of everyone.

He was on high, and high above, He set up his court. They of his court were the animals and also his guard. Spider, A-nan-se, was their captain.

One day, Ananse asked Wulbari for a corncob.

"Of course," said Wulbari. "But what do you want it for?"

"Master, I will bring you a bushel of corn if you give me the corncob."

Wulbari had to laugh, and He gave Ananse the corncob.

Ananse made his way down the heaven road to the earth. He found a place to stay with a chief and asked where he could put the cob to keep it safe while he slept.

"It is the corn of God Wulbari," Ananse said. "And I must guard it."

So the people showed Ananse a good place in the roof for safekeeping.

During the night when all of them slept, Ananse took the corn and fed it to the chickens.

The next day, he made a great fuss about the missing corn. So the chief gave him a whole bushel of corn.

That was the way it was with Ananse. He could trick all of the people. He did it many times.

Once, he brought Wulbari a hundred men. Naturally, Ananse started to boast that he had more sense than God.

Wulbari heard this and called his captain to Him.

"You must go and bring me *something*," Wulbari told Ananse.

Ananse had no idea what *something* was.

That evening Ananse went to God for more information. But Wulbari only laughed.

"You say you are as good as I, so now prove you are My equal."

Next day, Ananse left the sky to find *something*.

Down on earth, he called all of the birds to him. And from each one, he took a fine feather. Then Ananse made a handsome robe of the feathers, which he put on. He took the sky road back to heaven and climbed to a top branch of a tree by the God's house.

When Wulbari came out and found the strangely colored bird, He called the animal people to Him.

"Do any of you know the name of this large, rainbow bird?" asked Wulbari.

None knew, not even the elephant, who knows all.

Someone said that Ananse might know. But Wulbari said He had sent Ananse to find *something*.

Everyone wanted to know what the something was. Wulbari told them.

"The *something* I wanted is the sun, and the moon, and the darkness," God said.

Everyone roared with laughter. They all left then, smiling over Wulbari's cleverness and Ananse's difficulty.

But Ananse, dressed as the bright-colored bird, had heard it all. Now he knew what *something* was. He took off his feathered coat and went far away. No one knows where Ananse went. But wherever it was, he found the sun and the moon, and he found darkness, as well. He put them all in his bag and went back to Wulbari.

Wulbari greeted him. "Well, and did you find *something*, Ananse?"

"Yes," Ananse said. He reached into his bag and drew out darkness. All went black, and no one, not even God, could see.

Next, he drew out the moon, and all could see just a bit.

At last, Ananse brought out the sun. Those who looked went blind. Those who had been looking somewhere else were blinded only in one eye. Some who had blinked right at the moment Ananse pulled out the sun were lucky and kept their eyesight.

So, you see, that is how blindness came into the world. That is because Wulbari had to have *something*. And Spider Ananse had the sense to get it for Him.

COMMENT: *This is an Ananse spider story from the Krachi people of Togo (formerly Togoland) in West Africa. Ananse is the trickster hero known by that name throughout West Africa. Under other names, he is still the great trickster all over Africa. The rivalry between him and the sky god is a popular story-telling*

device, and the weak (spider) overcoming the strong (sky god) is
an endlessly amusing motif. In the above creation myth, only the
god has power. Ananse must seek the advantage by means of his
wit and trickery. He is successful in tricking the god and his court
into thinking he is a bird. Then he overhears what something *is,*
and by finding darkness, moon, and sun, Ananse proves
he is equal to God Wulbari.

Water and the Animals That Live in It

THE WOMAN WHO FELL
FROM THE SKY

Divine Woman the Creator

In the beginning, there was only water and the water animals that lived in it.

Then a woman fell from a torn place in the sky. She was a divine woman, full of power. Two loons flying over the water saw her falling. They flew under her, close together, making a pillow for her to sit on.

The loons held her up and cried for help. They could be heard for a long way as they called for other animals to come.

The snapping turtle came to help. The loons put the woman on the turtle's back. Then the turtle called all the other animals to aid in saving the divine woman's life.

The animals decided the woman needed earth to live on.

Turtle said, "Dive down in the water and bring up some earth."

So they did that, those animals. A beaver went down. A muskrat went down. Others stayed down too long, and they died.

Each time, Turtle looked inside their mouths when they came up, but there was no earth to be found.

Toad went under the water. He stayed too long, and he nearly died. But when Turtle looked inside Toad's mouth, he found a little earth. The woman took it and put it all around on Turtle's shell. That was the start of the earth.

Dry land grew until it formed a country, then another country, and all the earth. To this day, Turtle holds up the earth.

Time passed, and the divine woman had twin boys. They were opposites, her sons. One was good, and one was bad. One was born as children are usually born, in a normal way. But the other one broke out of his mother's side, and she died.

When the divine woman was buried, all of the plants needed for life on earth sprang from the ground above her. From her head came the pumpkin vine. Maize came from her chest. Pole beans grew from her legs.

The divine woman's sons grew up. The evil one was Tawis-karong. The good one was Tijus-keha. They were to prepare the earth so that humans could live on it. But they found they could not live together. And so they separated, with each one taking his own portion of the earth to prepare.

The bad brother, Tawis-karong, made monstrous animals, fierce and terrifying. He made wolves and bears, snakes, and panthers of giant size. He made mosquitoes huge, the size of wild turkeys. And he made an enormous toad. It drank up the fresh water that was on the earth. All of it.

Turtle and Earth

The good brother, Tijus-keha, made proper animals that were of use to human beings. He made the dove, and the mockingbird, and the partridge. And one day, the partridge flew toward the land of Tawis-karong.

"Why do you go there?" Tijus-keha asked the partridge.

"I go because there is no water. And I hear there is some in your brother's land," said the partridge.

Tijus-keha didn't believe the bird. So he followed, and finally he came to his evil brother's land. He saw all of the outlandish, giant animals his brother had made. Tijus-keha beat them down.

And then he saw the giant toad. He cut it open. Out came the earth's fresh water. Tijus-keha didn't kill any of his brother's creations. But he made them smaller, of normal size so that human beings could be leaders over them.

His mother's spirit came to Tijus-keha in a dream. She warned him about his evil brother. And sure enough, one day, the two brothers had to come face to face. They decided they could not share the earth. They would have a duel to see who would be master of the world.

Each had to overcome the other with a single weapon. Tijus-keha, the good, could only be killed if beaten to death with a bag full of corn or beans. The evil brother could be killed only by using the horn of a deer or other wild animal. Then the brothers fixed the fighting ground where the battle would begin.

The first turn went to the evil brother, Tawis-karong. He pounded his brother with a bag of beans. He beat him until Tijus-keha was nearly dead. But not quite. He got his strength back, and he chased Tawis-karong. Now it was his turn.

He beat his evil brother with a deer horn. Finally, Tijus-keha took his brother's life away. But still the evil brother wasn't completely destroyed.

After he died, Tawis-karong came to Tijus-keha, appearing before him.

"I have gone to the far west," he said. "All the races of men will follow me to the west when they die."

It is the belief of the Hurons to this day. When they die, their spirits go to the far west, where they will dwell forever.

COMMENT: *The Hurons are a confederacy of American Indians originally of the St. Lawrence Valley. This creation myth falls into the* Earth-Diver *category. In this type of myth, a being—sometimes divine, often an animal—dives into the water to bring up small amounts of soil. From this soil, the earth is formed.*

Nyambi

MAN COPIES GOD

Nyambi the Creator

In the beginning, N-yam-bi lived on earth with his wife, Nasi-lele. As god, he made the birds and all of the animals and fishes.

One thing Nyambi made was different, and it was man. The first man's name was Ka-mon-u. Kamonu liked to do everything Nyambi did. Kamonu worked wood when Nyambi did. He forged iron when Nyambi forged iron. Having the man copy him all of the time made Nyambi afraid.

One long day, Kamonu fixed a spear for himself. He killed an antelope, and he did not stop there. He killed again and again.

"Man!" Nyambi shouted. "What you do is wrong. You are killing your brothers."

So Nyambi took Kamonu away to another region. But Kamonu came back. Nyambi let him come; to calm man, he gave him a place to plant and to grow things.

Well, one night, there were buffalo wandering around in Kamonu's garden. Kamonu took his spear and killed them. Then there were antelope who strayed into his garden. Kamonu killed them as well.

One day, Kamonu's pot suddenly broke. His dog died. Then his child was dead, too. Kamonu hurried to tell Nyambi. But when he got there, Kamonu found his child unharmed, his dog barking and wagging its tail, and his pot as good as new.

"Give me some of your magic power, great Father," Kamonu said.

But Nyambi wouldn't give him any.

Nyambi said to his aides, "How can I keep Kamonu from coming here to bother me?"

They told him only god would know. And he, Nyambi, was god.

So Nyambi moved his family and people across the river. But Kamonu made a raft and came over.

Nyambi made a mountain and lived at the very height of it. Kamonu found his way up there, too. And all this time there were great numbers of human beings growing and living on the earth.

Nyambi sent out birds to look for a place for him to get away. They found nothing.

Next, a seer told him to go find Spider. He did that. Spider found a place for Nyambi up in the sky.

"How do I get up there?" Nyambi asked.

"You climb this," said Spider. And he spun a fine thread from the earth way up to the sky.

Nyambi climbed up all the way to the sky on this very long thread. The seer told him he'd better put out Spider's eyes, or

Spider could show Kamonu the way to heaven. So Nyambi did put out the eyes of Spider.

That is how Nyambi vanished from earth and was gone into the sky.

Kamonu said to some men, "We must make a great pile that will reach to the top up there."

He and the men did that. They chopped trees down. They cut logs, and they piled the logs one upon the other, higher and higher, so they could climb up to Nyambi. The pile went almost to the sky; it was that high. But it wouldn't stand up; it was too heavy. Suddenly the logs rolled away, and the pile fell down.

The first man, Kamonu, was not able to find a way to Nyambi in the sky. But every morning when the sun came up, Kamonu gave it his greeting.

"There rises Nyambi," he said. "Our god has come!"

COMMENT: *This myth from the Lozi people of Zambia is called a* Divine Myth. *In this type of myth, god simply is there, and is god, and creates earth and all that is human. It includes the often comic situation of having men at odds with the will of god.*

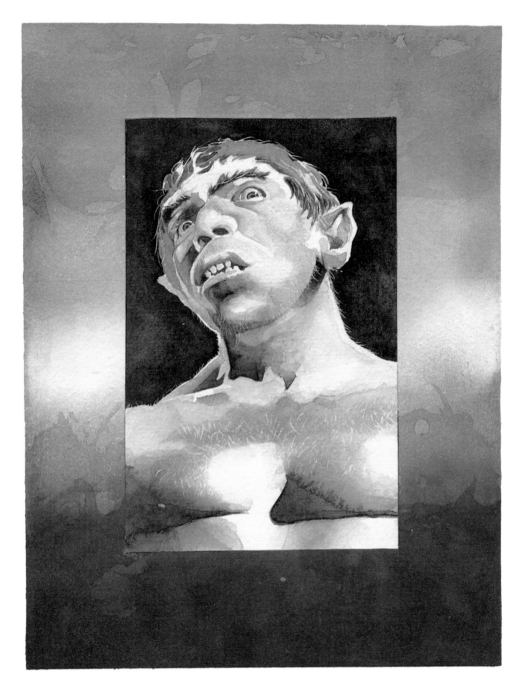

Imir

THE FROST GIANT

Imir the Creator

In the beginning, there were two realms. Muspell was in the south, and it was full of fire and blinding light. Niflheim, the home of fog, ice, and snow, lay in the north.

Between the two realms was a vast stretch of empty space called Gin-nun-ga-gap, or Yawning Gap. Warm air drifted from Muspell and mixed with the cold from Niflheim, the north realm. This breath of summer and winter met in a thaw above the middle realm of Yawning Gap. The drips and drops started life growing. And life took the form of a great giant. His name was Imir. And from the beginning, he was evil.

Imir was a frost giant. He lay down to sleep in Yawning Gap and sweated through the night. A woman and a man grew from his armpit. A son came forth from his leg. From Imir came the first family of ice-crusted frost giants.

Melting ice from the middle realm of Yawning Gap formed into a giant cow. Imir drank the rivers of milk from the cow. The cow lived off the ice itself. She licked and licked blocks of it.

A man's head appeared from one block. For three days and nights the cow fed on the ice block. And finally a whole man was born from it. He was called Buri, so tall and strong.

Soon Buri had a son he called Bor. Bor married a daughter of a frost giant, and they had three sons. These were the gods Odin, Vili, and Ve.

The god brothers hated the evil Imir and the ever-growing number of brutal frost giants. They attacked Imir and they killed him. Imir bled, and the blood drowned all of the frost giants except two. The two got in a hollow tree trunk and rode away on a blood tide.

Odin, Vili, and Ve carried the dead Imir to the middle of Yawning Gap. They made the world from his body. The earth was shaped from his flesh. Mountains were formed from his bones. Rocks, stones, and boulders came from his teeth and jaws.

After they had formed the earth, Odin, Vili, and Ve took the blood that was left from Imir and made the ocean in a ring.

The three brothers lifted the skull of Imir and made the dome of the sky. They placed a dwarf at each of the four corners to support the sky high above the earth.

Then the gods went to the southern realm of Muspell and took sparks and embers. From these they made the sun, moon, and stars. They placed the sun, moon, and stars way up over Yawning Gap to light up both heaven and earth.

Odin and Vili and Ve were walking one time at land's edge where it met the sea. They saw an ash tree and an elm tree, both fallen down. The three brothers lifted them and created from them a new man and woman. Odin breathed life into the man and woman. Vili gave them wit and feelings. Ve brought them hearing and sight.

The man's name was Ask, and the woman was Embla. The brothers gave them the land of Midgard as their home. Midgard was protected from the giants' world by a wall made from the eyebrows of Imir.

So it is that all nations and all families and every race of human beings came from Ask and Embla. They were the first of their kind in the new world created by Odin, Vili, and Ve, the sons of Bor.

COMMENT: *This is a small section of the* Prose Edda, *an Icelandic epic written down in 1220 by Snorri Sturlason (1173–1241), the great poet, historian, and critic. It was written possibly from narratives and summaries of lost, ancient poems. The first part of this myth tells about the birth of the giant. The world is created from his body.*

Ask, the name of the first man created from a fallen tree, means ash tree. Embla, the name of the first woman, means elm tree.

Olorun and the Other Gods

OWNER OF THE SKY

Olorun the Creator

O lorun was the Owner of the Sky and the Highest
Being. He lived in the sky with other spirits. In the
beginning, the earth was all watery, just a marshy
place, a waste.

Sometimes, Olorun and the other gods came down to play
about in the marsh-waste. There were long spiders' webs hanging
from the sky. They draped across sweeping spaces like graceful
silk bridges.

Yet there was no solid land anywhere. No ground on which
to stand. There could be no human beings under the sky until
there was a hard place for them to plant their feet.

Olorun, Owner of the Sky and the Highest Being, called the
chief of the divine ones to him. This chief was Great God.

Olorun told Great God, "I want you to make some firm
ground down below, right away. Here," Olorun went on, "take
this."

He gave Great God a shell. There was a small amount of

earth in the shell. And there was also a pigeon in there and a hen with five toes.

Great God did as he was told. He went down to the marsh land, sliding down the spider silks. Then he threw the earth out from the shell and spread it about him. He put the pigeon and the hen down on the bit of earth from the shell.

The pigeon and the hen began scratching and scratching the earth with their feet. It didn't take long for them to scratch the soil over the whole marsh-waste. That was how the firm, hard ground came to be.

Great God went back up to the sky. There he found Olorun waiting.

"It is done. I've formed the ground, and it is solid and true," Great God said.

Olorun sent down Chameleon to take a look at the work of Great God.

Now, Chameleon took his time about most things. He walked slowly, and he went down the spider line from the sky carefully. He rolled his big eyes around, looking at everything. And slowly he changed his color from sky blue to earth brown as he walked the land Great God had made.

"Well, the earth is plenty wide," Chameleon told Olorun when he had returned, "but it's not quite dry enough."

"Go again," Olorun commanded. And Chameleon went down from the sky a second time.

He came back to report once more to the Owner of the Sky.

Chameleon

"It is well," Chameleon said. "The earth is wide, and it is dry this time."

"Good," Olorun said. He named the place Ifé, and that meant wide. Ile was brought to stand on Ifé, and Ile meant house. All other houses came from that first one that stood at Ifé. And to this day, the city of Ile-Ifé is the most sacred to Olorun's people.

It took four days to make the earth. On the fifth day, Great God was to be worshipped as the Maker.

Then Olorun sent Great God back to Ifé to plant trees and to feed humans when they came, and to give them goods. He planted palm trees with palm nuts. The humans would drink their juice. More trees were planted there, and rain was made to fall and water them.

The first people came from heaven. Olorun sent them down to earth to live. Great God made some of the people's parts out of the earth. He molded their bodies and their heads.

Bringing these still figures to life was left to Olorun, Owner of the Sky, the Creator.

Great God was jealous of Olorun's work. He wanted to bring life to the earth figures he had made.

"I will watch Olorun to see how he does it," thought Great God.

So he stayed there with the figures and hid amongst them so that he might see the work of Olorun firsthand.

But Olorun knew everything. He knew whenever there were

watchers. He saw Great God there where he had hidden. And he put Great God into a very deep sleep.

Great God slept and slept. When he woke up again, all of the people had come to life. He never saw it happen.

So it is that Great God still only makes the bodies and heads of humans, both men and women. He leaves his marks on them, though. And sometimes, the marks show how unhappy Great God is.

COMMENT: *In this primal myth of the Yoruba of Nigeria in Africa, the Supreme Being, Olorun, is the Owner of the Sky, the Creator. Myths told about him explain the origins of the world and human beings.*

Although he is the greatest of the gods, he is a god who keeps his distance. There is a Yoruba proverb: "A man cannot cause rain to fall, and Olorun cannot give you a child." This function of providing children is given to one O-ba-ta-la, who is the chief god of the Yorubas. Olorun handed Obatala the world and the heaven and then withdrew himself.

In the above myth, there is no mention of Obatala and the lesser gods of the Yoruba people. However, it is Obatala who sends children to parents. But Olorun alone owns the sky. He also owns the sun, for orun *as in Olorun, means sky and sun both.*

Apsu the Begetter

MARDUK, GOD OF GODS

Apsu and Tiamat the Creators

What was on high had not been named. And firm ground below had not been called. There was but Apsu the begetter, the fresh and sweet-water sea. And there was Tiamat, the salt-sea waters. They mingled as a single body and soul.

There was no hut of reeds. No marsh lands. When there was Apsu and Tiamat, and nothing else, they created the great gods.

They brought the gods Lahmu and Lahamu into being. And for ages these two grew and grew.

The gods Anshar and Kishar were formed next, and they grew even taller. The god Anu was their son. He was equal to his father, Anshar.

Anu brought the god, Ea, into being. Ea was wise, understanding, and strong. He was even mightier than his grandfather, Anshar. There were none to rival him among the gods.

The god brothers banded together in the sweet and salt waters as more of them came into being. They surged back and forth. This bothered Tiamat. Some say she was a dragon. The god sons made her moody with their noise and laughter.

Apsu could not stop the brother gods, and Tiamat could not speak to them, for they were too overbearing. Apsu decided to destroy them so that he and Tiamat could have peace.

"What? Should we unmake what we have made?" Tiamat asked. Her mood was dark now. "Their ways are awful, these gods, but let us act kindly!"

Apsu continued to plan evil against the gods, his sons. But the gods heard what was plotted. They became silent, all but one. He was Ea, the all-wise.

Ea made a spell. He spoke the magic, and he put it in the deep of the fresh water that was Apsu. His spell made Apsu fall sound asleep, and then Ea killed him.

Ea and Damkina, his wife, dwelled in splendor in this watery place of fate; they called it the Apsu. And in the heart of the Apsu was created the majestic god, Marduk. It was Ea and Damkina's doing. They were the father and mother.

Marduk looked like a god of gods for all time. His eyes flashed and sparked. Leader that he was, he walked like a Lord of the Ages. When Ea first saw him, his heart was filled with rejoicing. He said Marduk was perfect and to be praised as the most high god.

Marduk had four eyes and four ears. When his lips moved, the fire blazed from within. His eyes scanned everything. He was fearless and radiant. He was best and tallest, boldest and brave.

"My little son, my little son!" exclaimed Ea. "My son, the sun! Sun of the Heavens!" Marduk was the sun of all.

The god Anu then made the four winds. They, in turn, brought waves and foam to Tiamat's waters. Diving down, Anu filled his palm and created dirt. Waves stirred up the dirt.

Tiamat did not like being upset and so disturbed. She moved and moved, day and night. The gods could not rest.

"We cannot sleep," they said. "You let Apsu be killed and did not stay at his side. Now there are four winds. You are alone. We cannot rest. You do not love us!"

"Let us make monsters, then!" Tiamat said.

She who could fashion all things gave birth to monster serpents. She made roaring dragons, bloodless and filled with poison. And she crowned them with haloes, so they would look like gods. Looking upon them, the onlooker would perish.

Tiamat created the Viper, the Dragon and the Sphinx, the great Lion, the Mad Dog, and the Scorpion Man. She created demons, the Dragon-fly, the Centaur. There were eleven of them that she made herself. And among these creatures she made Kingu.

Tiamat made Kingu the chief of the monsters, and they would battle now against the fairer gods—Anshar and Ea, and Anu. They would avenge the death of Apsu.

Anu went to stand against Tiamat and her terrible dark brood.

But Anu could not withstand her. He had to retreat.

Then Ea called his son, Marduk. And Lord Marduk was

Marduk

pleased. He prepared himself and stood before the fair god Anshar.

"I will accomplish all that is in your heart," said Marduk. "I will be your avenger and slay Tiamat. But you must make me supreme. From now on, my words will fix the destinies of the gods. And whatever I create will remain unchanged."

So the gods agreed to grant Marduk kingship of the universe. But first they spread the starry robe of the night sky in their midst.

The gods said to Marduk, "By your word, make the robe vanish."

Marduk spoke in words of sun and light, and the robe vanished.

"By your word," said the gods, "let the robe appear again."

Marduk spoke in the words of night and stars, and the robe was seen again.

The gods rejoiced.

"Marduk is King!" they said.

Then Marduk made ready for battle. He took up his scepter the gods had given him, his royal ring, and his thunderbolt. He took up his bow and arrow and his club. He placed lightning in front of him and made his body full of flame. He made a net to trap Tiamat.

The four winds helped him so that she could not get away. He brought evil winds, whirlwinds and hurricanes, to stir up the waters of Tiamat. He rode his terrifying chariot of rage. To this he tied his four-team: the Killer, the Crusher, Unyielder, and Fleet.

Lord Marduk went forward wrapped in armor, his head dressed in a turbaned halo. He went to face fierce Tiamat. He had magic in his mouth and a root against poison in his hand. The gods milled all around him. He went forward and looked inside of Tiamat.

"You have put Kingu in place of the rule of Anu and against Anshar, king of the gods. Stand up now and fight me!"

Tiamat cried out in fury. She cast her spells. The Lord Marduk spread his net to entrap her. She screamed out a poison. Then Marduk unleashed an evil wind. Tiamat spread her mouth to eat him. He drove the evil wind down her waterspout. Marduk let loose his arrow; it cut Tiamat in half.

Lord Marduk stood above Tiamat as she died. Her monsters and demons trembled with terror. Marduk captured them and smashed their weapons. When these dark gods cried out, Marduk crushed them underfoot.

Turning back to cold Tiamat, Marduk raised one half of her on high. He made it the heavens. Then he surveyed the Apsu of Ea, his father, and the deep waters. The other half of dead Tiamat he made the Earth, as a great abode above the Apsu.

Marduk the Victorious made the days of the year, and the order of the planets, and the moods of the moon. He made constellations of the gods.

He stood still for an age, having a strange and wondrous throught. He told Ea, his father, "I will have blood all around us. I shall frame it with bone. I shall build a creature.

"*Man* shall be his name!" spoke Marduk. "Oh, Man! You shall serve all of the gods."

And so it came to pass. The Lord God Marduk spoke it.
He let there be Man and thus freed the gods
from eternal labor.

COMMENT: *This myth is taken from the stunning Babylonian creation verse narrative,* Enuma elish, *perhaps the most famous of the Near Eastern texts. It symbolizes unity from which all life begins, and it also represents a* World-Parent *myth type. Apsu and Tiamat are not only ancestors of the gods, they also symbolize the living, unformed matter of the world.*

One of the purposes of the Enuma elish *was to praise Marduk, who was the main god of Babylon—to establish him as supreme, and to honor Babylon as the highest city.*

The Enuma elish *was discovered in the ruins of King Ashurbanipal's library at Nineveh dating back to 668–626 B.C., but it has been traced back to the First Babylonian Dynasty, 2050–1750 B.C., and the age of King Hammurabi, 1900 B.C., and even further back to the Sumerians who lived in the region before the Babylonians. The narrative takes its name from the first line: "Enuma elish la nabu shamanu . . . ," meaning "When on high the heaven had not been named . . ."*

Feathered Serpent

FOUR CREATIONS TO MAKE MAN

Maker and Feathered Serpent the Creators

The Word began long ago in a place called Quiché where the Quiché people lived. We shall tell how mysteries came out of shadows, out of the past. These things were brought to light by the Maker and Former, who had many names: Hunter Possum, Hunter Coyote, Feathered Serpent, Heart of Sky, Heart of Earth, Grandfather, Grandmother. . . .

There was once the ancient Book of Wisdom, written a long, long time ago. It is a great story about the birth of heaven and earth. There were four creations. Here is the telling of all of these things. . . .

The First Creation

There was no one, at first. There was not one animal, yet, and no bird, fish, or tree. There was no rock or forest, no canyon, no meadow.

There was sky separated from all things. The face of the earth was invisible. There was nothing that could make a sound.

There was the sea, so calm and all alone. There was dark and night and sea murmurings, ripplings. Yet within the dark and night and sea, there was the Maker and there was the Feathered Serpent.

Maker and Feathered Serpent came together. They were in the calm water, and They were brilliant, They glittered with all light. They were there, wrapped in blue and green feathers.

They were the great thinkers. And so it is that there was sky and the Heart of Sky. Thus is God, and so He is called.

Behold the Heart of Sky and His three signs: Lightning Hurricane, New Lightning, and Blue-green Lightning.

And They, the three flashes who were the Heart of Sky, came to Feathered Serpent.

And came the word of God, spoken with Maker and Feathered Serpent. Together They thought and figured out. All of Them discussed what must be done to bring life and light. What would light be and dawn? Who would bring food? Who would provide?

And They brought Their words together, joined them with Their thoughts, planned creation. Their words and thoughts were so clear that whatever They said came to be.

"Let it be that water should go, be emptied," They said. "There will then be the plate of earth to be made ready for sowing and brightening and warming."

They created earth by saying it.

"Earth," They said. "Earth!"

And there it was suddenly, forming out of dust and mist.

"Mountains and valleys," They thought.

Their magic and power brought trees to cover the mountains.

"Pines!" They said, and pines came to be.

Feathered Serpent was pleased.

"I'm glad You have come, oh Heart of Sky," It rejoiced, "Lightning Hurricane, New Lightning, Blue-green Lightning."

So the earth was readied as They were first in the universe to think of each thing and say it. Sky and earth were parted and made perfect.

Next They thought of wild animals to guard the forest.

There would be deer and birds, panthers and serpents. Deer and panthers would walk on four feet.

There would be places for all of them, in the trees and thickets, in the bushes, in the hollows and caves so they might rest and sleep and stay.

The wild animals, the First Creation, were told by God:

"Speak, don't mutter or cry out. Talk, each one to each one, to each kind, to each group of you.

"Say Our names, praise the God. We are Mother and Father. Speak to Us as who We are—Lightning Hurricane, New Lightning, and Blue-green Lightning, Heart of Sky, Maker, Feathered Serpent."

But the deer and the birds, the panthers and serpents just rustled; they rattled and roared and howled and warbled. They just twittered and chattered; they could not talk like men, like humans. They would not. They all cried out in different sounds. There was no language.

Maker heard and said, "They can't say Our names. They can't praise Us. We are their makers, and We will have to begin again."

So the God said to First Creation, "You do not speak, so We will change you and remake you.

"As you are now, you are brought low. You will serve, you will not lead.

"You—bird, deer, you will stay where you are, where you sleep and eat, in the forests and canyons, among tree and bush. You will be eaten, you will kill and be killed. You will stay low and serve, since you cannot talk and praise your God."

So it was tried again. The Word. And quickly, because the planting time was coming, the brightening time.

The Second Creation

Maker tried again to create a praisegiver and foodbringer.

This time the human form was made out of the wet earth, out of mud.

They who were God made the body, but it looked bad, not good. It fell apart, it was so damp and watery. It didn't look at Them who made it. It had a face on one side of its head. It made no sense when it tried to speak.

Animals of the First Creation

"It can't walk," said Maker. "It can't make more of itself. It won't last, it will just get wetter."

So They let Second Creation melt on the watery sea. Only the thought of it was left.

Then They made another plan to create man, so they could have praise and prayers.

This next man would be carved from wood.

"Find it, and carve it, and shape it. Fix it with corn and red bean. "Make it carved of wood," said Heart of Sky and Feathered Serpent.

The Third Creation

"See," They said of the Third Creation, "It turns out nicely. It can speak."

And so it was that men were made carved of wood. They were wood models. They looked as people look. They walked. They talked; they multiplied. The earth was full of them. There were sons and daughters.

But . . .

Theirs were no minds. Theirs were no hearts. Theirs were no memories of the Maker. They did not remember the Heart of Sky and Feathered Serpent.

But . . .

They were the first numbers of people covering the earth. They were as wood dummies. They were just the model, then, for humankind. Their arms and legs were too thin, too wooden.

Man of the Third Creation

So the Heart of Sky brought a flood down on them. It was a great flood made to destroy them. And they were broken up.

Into the houses of the wood ones, what was left of them, came the animals of the forest, the First Creation. All of them came, big and small. They turned on the carved ones. They gouged them and gnawed them and tore them and crunched them.

Their dogs told the wood ones, "You caused us pain, you ate us. Now we will eat what is left of you."

And they did. Some of the wood ones escaped to the forest. You can see them still, living up in the trees. They are monkeys. That is why monkeys look so human. They are what is left of the wood dummies who could not think, could not walk straight, and were destroyed.

The Final Creation

Here begins true man's beginning and the search for that which would make his body.

And Maker, Heart of Sky, and Feathered Serpent spoke.

"The dawn has come. Morning has come for people of the earth."

And here the thoughts of Maker came in light. The sun, moon, and stars were coming soon. And They, the All-God, pondered as to what should make human flesh, and where it should come from.

As they thought and thought, four animals came to them:

What is Left of the Wood Dummies

mountain cat, coyote, little parrot, and crow. These four came from Broken Place, where yellow corn and white corn were plentiful. And these corns would be the human design, with water as blood. These would flesh out the formed and shaped people, the Final Creation.

The animals showed Them the way to get there.

Maker was joyful to find this mountain overflowing with yellow and white corn ears. And there were also honey and sweetest foods, fruit and vegetables. Small and great plants there, too.

The white and yellow corn was ground to fill many bushels, and with water there came human fat.

Maker and Feathered Serpent said:

"Making the first mother and father, We use yellow corn with white corn to build the flesh. We use food for the legs and arms of humankind."

"These will be the first fathers, the original four who are men."

And these are the names of the first humans who were formed:

> First is Jaguar Quiché.
> Next is Jaguar Night.
> Third is Ma-hu-cutah.
> Last is Wind Jaguar.

These are the names of our forefathers. Formed and shaped, never born of a mother; had no father, they are themselves great ones. Formed by Maker and Feathered Serpent.

And they were human. The four humans. They talked; they saw. They heard and listened. They worked and walked.

They looked good, and they were good humans. They were handsome. They saw all at once. They knew everything under the heaven. As soon as they looked at the earth and sky, they knew all very deeply.

They could see through trees and rocks, they could see through people.

Oh, those four were the best and the first: Jaguar Quiché, Jaguar Night, Mahucutah, and Wind Jaguar.

Maker asked them, "Do you know? Do you look? How good is your speech?"

The four beings saw everything under the sky clearly and perfectly. They gave thanks to Maker.

"Praise be, thanks to You, having formed us, three times thanks to have made us. We see what is far and near, what is great and small, up and down. We have mouths, and we can talk. Thank you, Grandmother, Grandfather."

"Well, that isn't good," Maker said. "You understand too much. You don't need to know everything perfectly."

So Maker took back some of it, took off a little of the vision that could see everything so clearly.

"Let it become like this," They, the All-God, said. "Since they are only Our designs, they shouldn't know or see too much. They are not God, but men only. So let them see only what is right near them. Let them be satisfied with sowing, and reaping, and borning.

"We'll take them apart somewhat. We'll weaken their eyesight so that close-up will be clear, but they won't see everything far away."

And the four humans were made to lose their complete knowing of all things. They knew some and a little more. But not everything, not like the Heart of Sky knew as God.

So it was that the Final Creation was done. The forming and making of the first grandfathers and fathers by the Heart of Sky and Heart of Earth.

And the mates to man came; their wives came into being by God's Word.

Sea House was the wife of Jaguar Quiché.

Fish House was the wife of Jaguar Night.

Hummingbird House was the wife of Mahucutah.

Parrot House was the wife of Wind Jaguar.

These were the names of the wives, and they were noble. They gave birth to the tribes, great and small—all of them.

There you have the root of us.

We, who are the Quiché people.

COMMENT: *The extraordinary* Popol Vuh *is the sacred history of the Quiché Maya, the once-powerful people of the highlands of Guatemala. In the early sixteenth century, the Quiché were con-*

quered and their religious books destroyed. The Popol Vuh *was rewritten in Latin script by a converted member of the tribe. That manuscript is lost. But a copy made and rendered into Spanish in the eighteenth century by Father Francisco Ximénez survives.*

The section of the Popol Vuh *above recounts the history of the Quiché through three distinctly flawed creations and one that is so perfect, it, too, is considered flawed and must be redone so that men will not be as perfect as god. It represents* Creation from the Word. *The God says "Earth!" and the earth comes into being.*

The earliest authors of this text were ancient Mesoamericans who lived in Central America in 950–1500 A.D. These were wise men and priests and members of ancient nobility. The theme of the whole Popol Vuh, *written over many centuries, tells of the greatness of the Quiché Mayan peoples, their sacred religion, and the rise and fall of things Quiché.*

Today, the people of Guatemala's highlands still speak a Mayan language. They say prayers to Mayan mountains and Mayan ancestors. And these Guatemalans tell time according to the Mayan calendar.

The Egg

THE ANGRY GODS

Ta-aroa the Creator

Ta-aroa lived alone in a shell shaped much like an egg. The egg revolved in dark, empty space for ages.

Then came a new time, and Ta-aroa broke out of the egg. Being so by himself, he made the god, Tu. Tu became Ta-aroa's great companion and helper in the wonderful work of creation.

Ta-aroa and Tu made gods to fill every place. They made the universe. And they brought forth land and creatures. Last, they created man to live on the earth.

The first man that was created was called Ti-i. Ta-aroa made him out of earth. He put sand on Ti-i for his clothing. Then Ta-aroa said to Ti-i, "You are perfect."

Next, a woman was made. She was Ti-i's wife, Hina, and she was half goddess and half mortal. Hina had a face both in front and in back. She was full of good, making hard things easy, and hurt less painful.

But first man Ti-i was mean and liked to see others suffer. He sent out a white heron to cast a spell over the world.

For a time after creation, there was peaceful quiet. But then unhappiness and unease came into the universe. The spell of the white heron was everywhere. The gods in their separate places started warring with one another and with men.

Ta-aroa and Tu spoke curses to punish them.

"We curse the stars!" they said. And the stars blinked.

"We curse the moon!" The moon faded and went out.

Hina thought to save the stars and the moon. Sure enough, the stars are still there, although they may twinkle and blink. And the moon may disappear, but it comes back a little at a time until it has all returned. That is because Hina was so good.

"We curse the sea!" spoke Ta-aroa and Tu. That caused low tide.

Hina saved the sea and brought high tide. Low and high tide have followed one another ever since.

"We curse the rivers!" Ta-aroa and Tu shouted. And the waters hid under the soil.

Hina brought back the terrified waters, making them bubble out of the ground to form springs, and they are there even today.

Ta-aroa and Tu cursed the trees. The leaves turned yellow; the fruit did not ripen on time. But Hina was always there, and she saved them. New leaves grew from the trees. And now the fruit ripens when it should.

"We curse mankind!" roared Ta-aroa and Tu. Humankind that was man and woman and children bowed low in fear.

Hina prepared to save their lives. She would have, too, had it not been for Ti-i. He used magic to conjure them to death.

"Oh, Ti-i," Hina said. "Do not try your blackest magic on them! When humanity suffers, you know I'll make it better.

"Look there," she said. "My moon and stars, my trees and fruit, are they not better than your cruelty?"

But Ti-i would hear nothing good.

"My master is Ta-aroa," spoke Ti-i. "You have seen how he loves to kill. It was he who made the people bow down."

So it is that the Tahitians say it was the man and not the woman who caused people to lose eternal life.

They also say this: It was not long before Ti-i fell and died beneath his own curse.

COMMENT: *This Tahitian myth from the Society Islands (French Polynesia) is known as a* cosmic egg *type. It is but one version of the myth that is also found on Samoa, two thousand miles west of Tahiti, where the god is called Tangaroa.*

The supreme being, Ta-aroa, which means unique, *exists within the egg and is thus the source of all life.*

The egg acts as an incubator.

Only the Ocean

SUN, LIFE, WIND, AND DEATH

God Lowa the Creator

In the beginning, long ago, there was only the ocean. Then the God Lowa came down, and he commanded; he caused a humming sound, and the Marshall Islands were made. He went back to heaven, and four men came to the island Ai-ling-lap-lap. They went in different ways—west, east, south, and north.

The man in the east brought light. He was the Sun. The one in the west had to see that all living things were made. He was Life. The man from the south looked after the winds. He was Wind. And the man in the north killed all things by single acts. He was Death.

When Sun, Life, Wind, and Death found their different directions, God Lowa sent a fifth man down to arrange the Marshall Islands. The fifth man put the islands in a basket and began placing them, one by one, in their proper order in the ocean.

As the man went from Ailinglaplap to Jaluit, one island, Namorik, fell. He let it slip out of his hand and never bothered to put Namorik back in the right order. To this day, it is still out of line.

Well, the man put Jaluit in the water, and Ebon, next. Then he threw away the basket! And the basket became the island, Kili. That finished the making of the Marshall Islands.

Then God Lowa sent down two men to Ailinglaplap to tattoo all that had been created—the birds and animals, fishes, humans, everything. Everybody on earth had to come to Ailinglaplap to be tattooed. That's how each kind of thing has its own markings. And that's why the highest-rank tattoos are for chiefs, and different ones are for women, and then commoners and animals.

One time a canoe came from Bikini Island. There were people and animals in it. It didn't have any sails, but there was a special part of the canoe called the "fish." This "fish" pushed the canoe to the island of Wotho.

There was a ghost on Wotho. It speared the "fish," making a hole in it. Then the people had to paddle all the way to Ailinglaplap. They paddled until they were so tired that nobody wanted to bail out the canoe.

At the south pass into the lagoon at Buoj, at the edge of the reef, the canoe sank. The people had to swim, the birds had to fly up, and all the animals had to swim to the shore. The rat was a very poor swimmer, and he almost drowned.

Rat was struggling along, struggling along, when Octopus came up from down under.

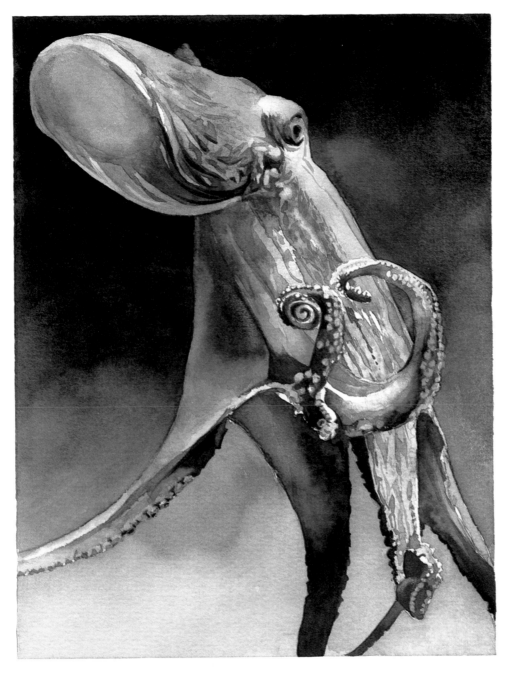

Octopus

He said, "Oh, my friend, let me help you."

Octopus put Rat on his head and took him to shore. Just before Rat jumped off, he did something on Octopus's head.

"Ha, ha, I put something up there!" Rat said.

Octopus felt his head and discovered something up there that he didn't want to touch or even wipe off. Octopus was so angry at Rat. He couldn't catch him, though, because Octopus can't walk on land. But to this day, he hates Rat.

Rat did finally get his tattoo. He was last to get one, and there was too much water in the tattoo dye by then. That's why Rat's tattoo looks weak, just a gray color. His markings make the rat look dirty, ratty. Especially since everybody else got a good tattoo.

Now everything in the world had its tattoo. All things had been given their names—fishes, men, women, and animals. It was up to the east man, Life, to see that everything got born and grew. South man, Wind, blew the clouds and made rain. And the north man that was Death called people just when he wanted them. The people were buried near the lagoon side of the atoll. After six days, souls rise from the grave to go to the islet, Nako. Before entering this islet, souls must cross a channel full of large fish. No soul escapes the jump.

Bad people, who are full of sin, can't make the jump over. They fall down, and the fish eat them. Good people easily get across. They have respected their mothers and fathers. Some of them have been brave in battle. And they have respected their chief. They reach the spirit island and are rewarded with everlasting fat of the squirrel fish. None of the good people are ever hungry or thirsty again.

From the spirit islet of Nako, people go to live with the north man, Death.

COMMENT: *The Republic of the Marshall Islands consists of the easternmost islands of Micronesia. They are scattered over 180,000 square miles of the Pacific Ocean. The Marshalls comprise two parallel chains of coral atolls, the Ratak, or Sunrise, to the east, and the Ralik, or Sunset, to the west. The chains include more than 1,200 islands and islets.*

The "God Lowa" myth was told in the 1950s by the Marshallese, James Milne. It expresses the dual world of heaven and earth, and the creator Lowa, who makes the Marshalls by commanding them to appear while he is humming. Here also are four divinities who control all that is living—Sun, Life, Wind, and Death. There is the added motif of "why things are as they are"— why the rat is gray, why Octopus hates Rat, etc. Good humans are rewarded with life everlasting. Sinners are weighted by their crimes. They fall into the ocean (chaos) and are eaten by the fishes.

God Ra

THE SUN-GOD AND THE DRAGON

God Ra the Creator

Ra was the first to be. "When I came into being," he said, "then being itself came into being." He spoke these words so they would not be forgotten.

God Ra's father was the waters called Nun. "I put together in Nun some of the things as weary ones," said Ra, "before I found a place I could stand. I was alone; I made every form."

Ra set himself under the horizon every evening.

Each night, he crossed the Underneath Sky in his boat. That was not easy, for the Underneath Sky was a dark and terrible place.

The dragon, Apophis, lived in the Underneath Sky. It waited to destroy God Ra. Each dark-time, the dragon whipped his green tail back and forth, and each time, Ra fought the dragon and his mighty tail with all of his strength.

Ra's power was felt. Even though the dragon, Apophis, lived on, the smaller forces of darkness and disorder out of him were slowly being overcome.

God Ra spoke these words:

"Many were the beings that came out of my mouth. This was before there was heaven, before earth came into being, and before the ground and creeping things were created. Then they, too, started into being."

God Ra next spat out the god of the air. "You will be called Shu," he said. He sputtered out the god that was moisture and said, "I name you Tefnut."

It was Ra's father, the waters called Nun, who raised Shu and Tefnut.

All of this time, Ra had but one eye. He sent it forth to be watchful of his children. And though the Eye was distant from them, it followed Shu and Tefnut down through the ages.

"I wept with pleasure over my children," said Ra. "Then I came into this land, and Shu and Tefnut brought me my Eye. And my Eye was angered. For in its place, I had made another eye, the eye I wept with. I called my second eye The Golden One."

Shu and Tefnut brought two more gods into being. They were Nut and Geb, and they were too closely connected.

Shu set them apart. He lifted the female, Nut, up with her own gods. Nut counted her gods and made them stars. And then Shu, the god of the air, let his arms support Nut. And his arms kept the heaven apart from Geb.

Geb stayed in the lower world and was the earth. And Ra took back his Eye that was angered. He put it in the center of his head to shine forever upon the earth.

Apophis

All of this time, men had come into being from the tears Ra had shed with his second eye. And from the roots of his two eyes, he made whatever lives among the creeping things of snakes and insects—plants of all kinds.

So it was that out of Shu and Tefnut came Geb and Nut. And when Geb and Nut were separated, the earth and sky were parted.

Geb and Nut, earth and sky, brought the lesser gods, Osiris, Isis, and Horus into being—and many others, one after another.

And after the Great God Ra had cried men, there came all of men's multitudes.

All of these lesser gods spoke in magic, and they destroyed any enemies of Ra by the charms of their speech. And it was God Ra who sent them out to overthrow the evil dragon, Apophis.

Finally, it was done. The words that were spoken were not forgotten. God Ra could say them far and wide:

"The dragon is the one fallen! He cannot see! I say that a curse is cast on him. I have swallowed his bones, and his bones are not. His skin is not. His name is not; his children are not. I say he is fallen and overthrown."

Therefore, each morning, God Ra comes up shining in all of his splendor on the other side of the world.

These are the words that shall be spoken and never forgotten:

Now and Forever, Ra, the Sun-God, rises in triumph,
and he sets the same.

COMMENT: *The myth of Ra, or Re, is taken from Egyptian Mortuary Texts and is part of a temple ritual. Some of the ritual was a dramatic presentation of the conflict between God Ra and the dragon, Apophis.*

The myth is thought to come from ancient Thebes. Although the papyrus on which it was written dates c. 310 B.C., *the myth itself is said to be much older.*

Instead of riding in a chariot, the Sun-God Ra traveled the heavens in a boat called Millions of Years, *starting in the morning in the east, and at sunset, disappearing into the underworld of the Underneath Sky. The lesser god Osiris was the moon-god and the Judge of the Dead. Isis was Osiris's sister and the patron goddess of women. Horus was the son of Osiris and Isis and the savior of mankind.*

Sedi and Melo

SEPARATION OF EARTH AND SKY

Sedi and Melo the Creators

The earth was the woman, Sedi, and the sky was Melo, the man. The two of them married. And when they married, it was feared that they would come together and crush what lay between them.

Between the earth and sky were men and animals, lesser creatures of the middle realm. All these met to talk about how they might save themselves.

Sedi-Diyor, greatest of the middle-realm men, caught hold of Melo and beat him hard. Melo, the sky, fled far up into the heavens. He left Sedi, the earth, behind.

As Melo went away, earth Sedi gave birth to two daughters. But she would not look at them, so sad was she about losing her husband.

So Sedi-Diyor, greatest of the middle-realm men, had to find a nurse for earth Sedi's children. He did find one, and the little daughters grew under her care. Light came from them, shining on everything. Day after day, the light grew brighter.

Time passed, and the nurse died. Sedi-Diyor buried her in the ground. The two girls cried for her, as though she were their mother. They wept so hard that they pined away and lived no longer. The light that had grown brighter ended with them.

Darkness was everywhere. The men and animals were afraid. They wondered why the children had cried themselves to death. Perhaps it was because the nurse had stolen from them. Men and animals dug in the ground where the nurse was buried to see what they could tell. But all they found were two great and shining eyes peering through the darkness. They saw their own reflection in the eyes.

Men took the eyes to a stream and washed them a long time. That made the eyes shine even more. Still, the men couldn't take away the images they saw looking out from the eyes.

So the men called for a carpenter. The carpenter came and worked on the eyes, taking out the reflections. These images became two girls. The men and animals called them Sedi-Irking-Bomong and Sedi-Irkong-Bong. They would not let them out of the house.

The girls grew up. One day Bomong, the oldest, got dressed up in bright clothing and pretty ornaments. She looked lovely, and she set out to wander through the world. As she fled from the house, light surrounded her. It was daylight. She walked away across the hills and never came back.

Finally her sister, Bong, went to find her. When she came out of the house, she brought more light. Light seemed to explode, breaking the rocks. It caused the trees to wither. Men fainted in the heat of the light.

The men and animals talked about it. They knew they could not stand so much light. And they decided that they would have to kill one of the sisters so there would be less light. They talked on and on because they were afraid to hurt one of the girls.

At last, a creature, the frog, said he would wait for the girl, Bong, to come by. And he settled himself along her way. When she did come, all shining so bright and beautiful, down the path, he took his bow and arrow and shot her. Very quickly, she died from her wound. Then it was not as hot. The light did not pierce and blind the eyes. The trees came back to life. And the men and animals were able to go about their work again.

Bong lay where she had fallen. Another one of the creatures, a rat, dragged Bong on his back. He took her to Bomong. The poor rat kept falling down, Bong was so heavy. And rats' legs have looked funny and out of shape ever since.

The creature took Bong to the river where Bomong would pass. When she came along, he showed the body.

Bomong cried and cried. Perhaps she, too, gave off too much light. She was afraid that now she would be killed. Bomong sat down and placed a very large stone on her head. The stone made a shadow over her, and the world grew dark.

Men and animals were again afraid. They went to search for the light, and they found nothing. It was then that one of the men caught a cock and sent it to find Bomong. The cock found Bomong after a long time. He begged her to come back.

"No," she said. "They killed my sister, and they will kill me. Tell them I will come only if they bring my sister back to life again."

"I will tell the man what you have said," spoke the cock. The cock went back, and he told the man.

The man got a carpenter to fashion a new Bong. The carpenter made Bong small. He put life into her body, and she became alive.

Bomong heard that her sister was now alive. She threw down the stone from her head. She stood, beautiful as ever. Light dazzled and spread out. The day returned.

The cock gave a cry, "kok-o-ko!"

All were glad there was light and heat in the
world once more.

COMMENT: *This is a creation myth of the Minyong, a tribal group in northeastern India. Out of fear, the younger gods conspire to drive out the father-heaven, Melo, producing darkness and chaos. But the powerful men and animals of the middle realm between earth and sky struggle to finally arrange things in order, enough to permit life and light. The animals of this story are not ordinary.*

They all speak and understand and take action. The tale has its own logic. We can assume that the carpenter made the new Bong small so that she would give off less light. At the end, the light of the two sisters is not so overpowering that it disturbs the men and animals. It is the steady daylight that allows life to continue and grow.

First Man, First Woman

FIRST MAN, FIRST WOMAN

Yahweh the Creator

On the day that Yahweh, the Lord God, made the earth and the heavens, no plant of the field was yet in the earth, and no herb of the field had yet sprung up. For the Lord God had not caused it to rain upon the earth, and there was no man to till the ground. But a mist went up from the earth and watered the whole face of the ground.

Then the Lord God formed man out of dust from the ground, and He breathed into his nostrils the breath of life; and man became a living being. And the Lord God planted a garden in Eden, in the east; and there he put the man whom He had formed. And out of the ground the Lord God made to grow every tree that is pleasant to the sight and good for food.

He made the tree of life, also, in the midst of the garden, and the tree of the knowledge of good and evil.

A river flowed out of Eden to water the garden, and there it divided and became four rivers. The name of the first is Pishon. It is the one which flows around the whole land of Havilah, where there is gold and onyx stone. The name of the second river is Gihon. It is the one which flows around the whole land of Ethiopia. And the name of the third river is Tigris, which flows east of Assyria. And the fourth river is the Euphrates.

The Lord God took the man and put him in the garden of Eden to till it and care for it. And the Lord God commanded Adam, the man, saying:

"You may freely eat of every tree of the garden. But from the tree of the knowledge of good and evil you shall not eat, for the day you eat from it, you shall die."

Then the Lord God said, "It is not good that the man should be alone; I will make a helper fit for him."

So out of the ground the Lord God formed every beast of the field and every bird of the air, and He brought them to Adam to see what he would call them. And whatever Adam called every living creature, that was its name. Adam gave names to cattle, and to the birds of the air, and to every beast of the field.

But for Adam himself there was still not found a fit helper. So the Lord God caused a deep sleep to fall over him, and while he slept, the Lord God took one of Adam's ribs and closed up its place with flesh. The rib which the Lord God had taken from Adam He formed into Eve, and He brought her to him. And Adam said:

"This at last is bone of my bones and flesh of my flesh.
She shall be called Woman because
she was taken out of Man."

COMMENT: *This version of the sacred creation of man and woman narrative is taken from the Holy Bible Old Testament, Genesis, Chapter 2, Verses 1–23; and from The First Book of Moses, (a) "The Garden of Eden," Chapters II, 4–III, Pentateuch, The Five Books of Moses.* Adam *is the Hebrew word for man used in the sense of human being and is derived from* adamah, *earth.*

Some biblical scholars say that this creation was written by "J," one of the four main authors of the Pentateuch. The Bible version starting at Genesis 2:4b is known as Yahwist (J) (Jehovah) Creation Cycle text, representing the mythology of ancient Israel and dates from the ninth century B.C.

The creation of man and woman follows in the Bible and the Pentateuch directly after the seven days of creation, and both creation narratives describe the creation of human beings—"male and female He created them." However, the "First Man, First Woman" story describes the creation of man and woman in much more detail.

Chaos

THE COMING OF ALL THINGS

The Greek Creators

In the beginning, there came Nothing, alone. It was sometimes called Chaos, or the Void. But it was Nothing, all the same.

Next appeared Earth, so the gods would have some place to stand. And then came Tartarus, the underworld. Eros, love, came into being. Of all the forever gods, Eros was most handsome. He made all others weak. His power was greater than the strength of all to resist him.

Out of Nothing came darkest Night and Er-e-bos, another part of the underworld. This was the first generation of gods. Night and Erebos gave birth to Day and Space.

Earth brought forth Heaven and the Sea. Heaven was as great as Earth and spread out above and beyond Earth to cover her with stars. Heaven was a place of rest for all of the gods. And then Earth gave birth to mountains—Mt. Olympus being the home of the gods. There were other high places where they would also go to play. And there were the homes of the goddesses and Nymphs living in these pleasant, forest heights.

With Heaven whom she adored, Earth brought the Titans, her children, into being. They were many. Ocean was one, with its surges and waves and currents. Hy-per-i-on and I-a-pe-tos were others, and Thea, Rhea, and Phoebe. All Heaven and Earth were their parents.

The youngest Titan was Kronos. He was bold and wild. But Kronos hated his father sky, the Heaven.

Earth next gave birth to three proud Cyclopes. Each had one eye in the center of his forehead. They would make the thunder and the thunderbolt for the great god, Zeus, one day.

Earth and Heaven had three more sons. Oh, these were ungodly giants, awful and powerful. They each had a hundred terrifying arms, swaying and wheeling every which way. Each body had fifty heads atop massive shoulders. What monsters they were!

From the beginning, Heaven hated his and Earth's children. So he hid them away down inside her secret folds and caves. He would not let them see light or let them out. And he greatly enjoyed this wicked work of trapping them in darkness.

But Earth cried out, she was so full to bursting deep inside her. And so she planned her own wicked trick.

"My children," Earth told them, "your father is mean and savage. If you will help me, we can get even with him—evil for evil. For it was he who started this crime."

Earth grieved for her love of Heaven, yet she urged her children to do vengeance and fight for their lives. Therefore she made a huge, gray flint sickle, and she showed her children how to use it.

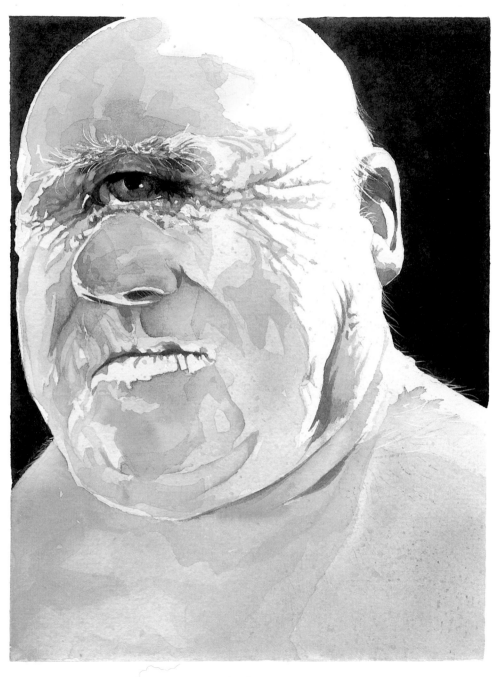

Cyclops

But they were all afraid, except for huge Kronos.

"Mother," he said, "I will do as you ask. I have no love for Heaven. He is no father to us, his children, since he began these terrible deeds."

Great Earth was happy with her awful son. She gave him the mighty sickle. She told him what to do, and she hid him so he could lie in wait for his father.

All Heaven came, bringing on the night and stars. Lovingly, he spread out over Earth. And as he did, bold Kronos struck with his sawtoothed sickle. He mowed down his father's love, and he dumped it into the sea. And from it, covered in foam, grew a woman, the goddess, Aph-ro-dīt-e.

Heaven cursed his children, saying they would be punished. But brave Kronos didn't care. He had his own children. Yet how could he trust even one of them? For Kronos knew what he had done to his own father, Heaven. And so, as his children were born from their mother, Rhea, Kronos ate them whole. He swallowed them up; he gulped them down! He did not want to end as his father had, to be one day overcome by one of his own.

Rhea begged Earth and Heaven to hide the new son who would now be born. This one would be called Zeus. And Earth and Heaven did hide the child after he was born. They hid him in Earth's vast, thick woods on Mt. Aegeum.

Rhea wrapped a giant stone in swaddling clothes. This covered stone she pretended was her newborn son, Zeus, and she presented it to awful Kronos.

Thinking it was real, Kronos seized the stone child. He swallowed it; it plopped hard in his belly. He had no idea his true son was safe and sound, hiding on Earth.

So it was that Zeus grew to be the greatest of the Gods, with Thunderbolt and Lightning as his aides. Zeus would one day conquer Kronos by force and power. He would drive him out of his place of honor. And then Zeus, Great God Zeus, would be father of all gods and all men.

COMMENT: *Hesiod's* Theogony *records the evolution of the Greek gods. It is an account of the origin and descent of the gods, and it establishes the Olympian order from which Zeus is triumphant.*

The Greek, Hesiod, lived in Boetia on the Greek mainland in the eighth century B.C. *In the above shortened version of the origin of the gods, the basic system is established. Nothing (chaos), Earth, Tartarus (the underworld), and Eros (love), simply appear. In the first generation, Nothing brings Night and Erebos into being. They, in turn, bring Day and Space. Earth gives birth to Heaven and the Sea by herself. Then Earth and Heaven bring forth the Titans. These and others later bring about the generation of the gods.*

Kronos (chronos) represented time to the Greeks. Kronos devoured his own children, and thus he (time) brought an end to all that had begun.

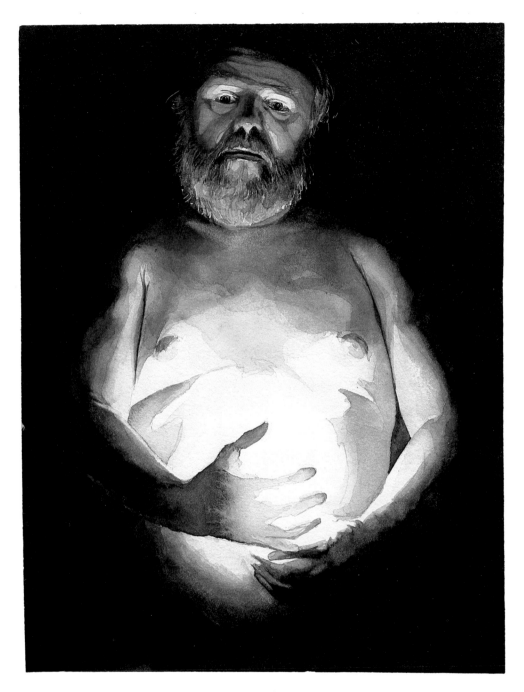

Prometheus

Prometheus the Creator

Pro-me-theus was wise. He was the grandson of Ocean, the Titan, and the son of Iapetos, who was brother to Kronos. Some say Prometheus was wisest of all the gods. His name means *forethought*.

Prometheus helped the Great God Zeus in the war against Kronos, the father of Zeus, and Kronos's brother Titans. The long battle nearly wrecked the universe before it ended. Kronos and the first generation of Titans were defeated.

Atlas, a brother of Prometheus, fought with the Titans. Later he was punished by Zeus, who made him hold the world and sky upon his shoulders forever. And so Atlas does to this day.

Epi-me-theus was also a brother of Prometheus. Epimetheus always followed the first idea that came to him. Often he changed his mind as the next idea came to him. The name Epimetheus means *afterthought*.

Epimetheus couldn't make up his mind about which side to take in the battle of the Titans against Zeus. So he did nothing and helped no one. Then again, he didn't hurt anyone, either.

Now, Prometheus and Epimetheus were to make men and all the animals. It was the will of the gods that they do so. Zeus didn't care, for the gods had made him their king, and the creation of lowly earth beings meant little to him.

It was decided that Epimetheus would make men and animals, and Prometheus would put on the final touches, so that there would be no mistakes.

Epimetheus made the animals first. He made birds, giving them wings so that they might test the wind. He gave them feathers to keep them warm, and he gave them keen eyesight so that they might see from the air where to find their food.

He made great bears with fur, and he made tiny creatures, also with fur and claws. He gave the bear and the little animals wildness and swiftness and a keen sense of smell. He gave the animals all he could think of—fierceness and strength, shells to some, great muscles to others.

Then it was time for Epimetheus to make men. He found he had nothing left that was good and strong to give to these humans. He had given all he could think of to the animals.

"You've done it again, brother," said Prometheus. "You've not thought out what you should do, but you've gone ahead, anyway, without thinking."

"What will happen to man?" cried Epimetheus. "Brother, can you help me?"

"Of course I can help you. But I will have to do the rest

of man, after you make the form in your making shop," said Prometheus.

And that is what happened. Epimetheus made new molds he fashioned in the shape of the gods. Prometheus mixed earth with water and made man in the image of the gods. Then Prometheus figured out a plan to make men better and wiser than the animals.

He went up to heaven, and when Zeus wasn't looking, he lit his torch there on the wheel of the sun's chariot.

"I'll give this heavenly fire to man," Prometheus told his brother when he returned. "With fire, man will have power over all animals. With fire, no animal will be a match for man."

And so it was that Prometheus stole fire and brought it down to man. With it, men could make weapons to fight and win over the animals.

Prometheus also gave wisdom to the forms Epimetheus had finished making. And with wisdom, men made tools with which to till the soil. They learned how to heat their homes with the fire, and this was how they were able to keep themselves warm. They next made tiny objects from metal. These were money used for trade.

Prometheus gave even more to man. At a place where men and gods came together called Field of Poppies, he saw to it that men got the best part of the animal sacrificed to the gods.

Prometheus planned this by making a sacrifice with a huge ox. He cut it apart and wrapped the meat with the entrails on top. Then he covered them in the beast's stomach pouch. Next, Prometheus put the bones in a pile wrapped in fat. God Zeus had to choose between the two piles of animal sacrifice.

Zeus knew well which was which. For he was the Great God and knew everything.

He had watched Prometheus steal fire for humans. That had been bad enough—not to ask permission and to place men above him, the Great God. But this trick was worse still. For Zeus knew well what Prometheus was thinking. The lesser part of the beast, the bone and fat, was meant for Zeus. This proved that Prometheus still favored humans above the Great God.

Ever after, gods got only bones from the sacrifice, while men ate all of the meat.

"I will teach Prometheus who is great," thought Zeus. "He will learn never again to trick me! First, I will punish man and Epimetheus. As for Prometheus, he will be punished last, and worst!"

So it came to be. Zeus fashioned something new up in heaven. All of the gods gave of themselves to make the new creation. Goddess Venus gave it beauty. God Mercury gave it persuasion. And God Apollo gave it music.

When the new creation was finished, Zeus wrapped it in innocence and sent it down to Prometheus and his brother, and to man.

"My creation will take care of all of them!" laughed Zeus.

It did take care. For it was woman made in heaven, and
she was lovely to behold.

COMMENT: *The Titans, often called the Elder Gods, were for
ages supreme in the universe. They were of enormous size and of
incredible strength. The most important was Kronos, and the
most fierce and forbidding was Zeus. The most famous was Prometheus. It was he who stole fire for man, thus placing men above
the god Zeus. Then Prometheus tricked Zeus with the fat of the
sacrifice, causing the god to take his fury out on Epimetheus and
men. Prometheus brought greater punishment from Zeus upon
himself. His tragic story can be found in Greek mythology.*

Pandora

PANDORA

Zeus the Creator

Pandora is the name of woman made in heaven. The name means "all's gift." After Zeus had wrapped her in a robe of innocence, other gods placed flowers in her hair.

Before Pandora left heaven, Zeus made the gods give her a box with a surprise inside.

"She won't be able to stop herself from looking in the box," Zeus said.

It was Apollo who gave Pandora the present from Zeus.

"The Great God sends this box," he said. Then he whispered to her, "Pandora, don't ever, ever open it!"

"Oh, I won't, if you say not to," she said to Apollo.

Pandora was so shy and as good as she could be. But she had one weakness which put a shadow in her eyes. She was curious about everything. Pandora had to look into all she saw. She had to touch this jar and that bottle.

"Oh!" she would exclaim, seeing something new. And she would peer under its cover and breathe deeply of its scent in order to know what it was.

"One look in the box, perhaps," she said to Venus, smiling her winning smile. "Just to see what might be inside?"

"No! No!" warned Venus. "Never, ever look inside the box!"

"Pandora, Zeus made us give it to you. He swore us to a terrible fate if we told you what was inside," Apollo said. "All we can do is give you fair warning."

"Yes, I heed the warning. I will not look," said Pandora. But she thought that somehow she must find a way to see what was inside the box.

Then Pandora was sent to Epimetheus, while his brother Prometheus was busy. She entered the house, and Epimetheus came upon her standing in the middle of the room, looking at everything. He could not believe his eyes. Pandora's beauty nearly blinded him.

"You are lovely!" he exclaimed. "No, you are perfect. No, you are more than perfect." He never could make up his mind. "You are a wonder to behold! Who are you?" he asked, falling in love with the vision before him.

"I am called Pandora," she said. "I come from Zeus, and I am to stay with you."

"Ah, Zeus!" said Epimetheus. "There must be a trick somewhere—the box! What do you carry in that box?"

"I don't know," said Pandora. "Zeus gave it to me."

"Never accept a gift from Zeus, my brother Prometheus warned me. The box must be an awful surprise. Here, I will put it away for you," said Epimetheus.

"Oh, no, I will keep it safe," said Pandora, in her sweet voice.

"Such beauty as yours cannot know the anger of Zeus," said Epimetheus.

He took the box out of her hands and carried it into his making shop. There he climbed on a stool and placed the box in shadow and on the highest shelf.

"Perhaps I should not have taken it," he muttered. "Oh, I'll give it back to her."

Suddenly he heard a muffled sound. The box seemed to shudder. "No, no, better leave it where it is." Quickly he shoved the box away and returned to Pandora.

He found her by the cupboard, looking into things. Epimetheus declared his love for her, and Pandora smiled. She said she would be pleased to share her time with him.

When Prometheus came home, he was angry with his brother. "Didn't I warn you never to accept anything, even a gift, from Zeus?"

"But you can't mean my beautiful wife, Pandora," cried the brother.

"I do mean her," said Prometheus. "Pandora in all her beauty was sent by Zeus to make us battle one another."

"It is the box that is the gift," said Epimetheus. "Not my wife."

Pandora was not really an evil trick from Zeus. He had meant her to be, but she was too good; all of the gods had seen to that.

But Pandora *had* to know more about the box. All of the days she was with Epimetheus, she waited for a time when both he and Prometheus were away. Then she wandered around the making shop. She looked at all the molds for making man that were now rusting, for man was made and doing well on earth. Finally her eyes rested on the box, high up on the shelf. She climbed the stool and stood on the very tips of her toes, but she could not reach the box.

"I know," she said, "I will put something sturdy on the stool, and then I will stand upon that."

Pandora found a small chest, which she sat atop the stool. She climbed up on the chest. Unsteadily, she stood on her toes, peering at the box.

"Just to bring it down and shake it and listen to it," she murmured to herself. "I won't open it. I promised I wouldn't."

She stretched as high as she could; her shaking hands reached the box. She slid it toward her. She tried to lift it, but it flew out of her hands, over the side of the shelf.

"Oh! Oh!" cried Pandora, stepping down before she, too, fell. The lid of the box came off and sailed through the air. The box tumbled. As it did, there was a great jumble of noise—roars and screams, howls and cries. For a moment the room was dark.

"What? Oh! No!" screamed Pandora.

For out of the box came awful things, the gifts of Zeus. Winged things and crawling things. Slithering things and creeping things, bringing with them a slime of dark and gray despair. Some

The Gifts of Zeus

creatures had pointed ears; some had flat, furry heads. Some had wicked eyes. Some were fanged, with scaly arms and hands. Some were tiny. Others were giant size. There were plagues of sorrow and pain. There was misery, holding its dripping head. Envy took hold of Pandora and tried to tear her hair out. Poverty slid hungrily across the floor and melted into the air.

Pandora flung herself at the box. She caught the lid and managed to fit it on.

But it was too late. All of the awful things were out of the box. They clamored through the house and on out into the street, the town, the whole world, it seemed.

There was one thing left quivering on the floor. It was a small thing. It must have been on the very bottom of the box. It was not as musty-smelling or as damp and horrible as the rest had been. To Pandora, its scent was quite sweet.

"You're not a bad one, I can tell," she said to it. "You're hurt, aren't you?" she asked it, swallowing her fear.

It didn't answer, so sick it seemed.

"Here, let me help you," she said. Pandora took hold of the thing by its wings. It felt warm, trembling. She could see its great heart swell and sink in its chest.

It sat up and rested against her.

"There, there," soothed Pandora. "That's better. Now tell me who you are."

"Ahhhh," sighed the thing. "I must go!" It rose weakly to its crooked feet.

Hope

"No, don't go," Pandora pleaded. "I need company. It is so lonely here."

"If I do not go, what will become of humans without me?"

"But who are you?" Pandora asked.

The thing smiled a wan smile. It seemed to gather strength within. Its brightly colored wings unfolded, bringing a fresh breeze.

"I am Hope," it said. "If I do not hurry, humans will have so little reason to live."

With one great leap, Hope sprang from the room, from the house, and into the world. Pandora stood at the door holding the empty box from Zeus in her hands. She saw Hope gather light around it, brightening the day.

"I let all of the ugly things out of the box," cried Pandora. "Human beings will have such trouble!"

She saw great Hope catch up to the ugly things of the world. When Hope was among them, the creatures seemed less sure of themselves.

So it was that hunger and poverty, despair and ugliness came into the world of humans. Forever and always, Epimetheus would have to live with Pandora, who had let one disaster after another out to torment life.

"Well, it's not all bad," Pandora thought. "There is always Hope!"

Hope stays in the world. It is the one good thing out of Pandora's gift box from the great, jealous God Zeus.

And what of Prometheus? His terrible punishment
was yet to come. But that is another story,
for another place.

COMMENT: *"Pandora" is one of the most famous of the Greek creation myths. Often she is portrayed as evil, although it is Zeus who supplies her terrible surprise. It should be noted that in some versions, Pandora's box is translated as a jar or chest. However, the most popular rendering of the gift from Zeus is a box. In one version, Pandora shuts Hope in the box forever. But it made more sense to this author that Hope should follow all of the horrors from the box into the world. By this contrast, Hope would make the world that much brighter.*

Let There Be Light

IN THE BEGINNING

Elohim the Creator

In the beginning, Elohim, God, created the heavens and the earth. The earth was without form. There was nothing, and darkness was upon the face of the deep. And the Spirit of God was moving over the face of the waters.

And God said, "Let there be light."

And there was light. And God saw that the light was good; and God separated the light from the darkness.

God called the light Day, and the darkness He called Night. And there was evening, and there was morning, one day.

And God said, "Let there be a vault in the midst of the waters, and let it separate the waters from the waters."

And God made the vault and separated the waters which were under the vault from the waters which were above the vault. And it was so. And God called the vault Heaven. And there was evening, and there was morning, a second day.

And God said, "Let the waters under the heavens be gathered together into one place. And let the dry land appear."

And it was so. God called the dry land Earth, and the waters that were gathered together He called Seas. And God saw that it was good.

And God said, "Let the earth put forth plants yielding seed, and fruit trees bearing fruit in which is their seed, each according to its kind, upon the earth."

And it was so. The earth brought forth plants yielding seed according to their own kinds, and trees bearing fruit in which is their seed. And God saw that it was good. And there was evening, and there was morning. It was a third day.

And God said, "Let there be lights in the vault of the heavens to separate the day from the night. And let them be for signs to mark seasons and days and years. And have them shine from the vault of the heavens to give light upon the earth."

And it was so. And God set two great lights in the vault of the heavens to separate the light from darkness. The greater light would rule over the day, and the lesser light would rule over the night. And God saw that it was good. And there was evening, and there was morning, a fourth day.

And God said, "Let the waters bring forth swarms of living creatures, and let birds fly above the earth across the vault of the heavens."

And God also created the great sea monsters and every living creature that moves, with which the waters swarm, according to their kinds, and every winged bird according to its kind. And God saw that it was good.

And God blessed them, saying, "Be fruitful and multiply, and fill the waters in the seas, and let birds multiply on the earth."

And there was evening, and there was morning. It was a fifth day.

And God said, "Let the earth bring forth living creatures according to their kinds; cattle and creeping things and beasts of the earth according to their kinds, and the cattle according to theirs. And everything that creeps upon the ground, according to its kind."

And God saw that it was good.

Then God said, "Let us make man in our image, after our likeness; and let them have dominion over the fish of the sea, and over the birds of the air, and over the cattle, and over all the earth, and over every creeping thing that creeps upon the earth."

So God created man in His own image, after our likeness, and He let them have dominion over the fish of the sea, and over the birds of the air, and over the cattle, and over all the earth, and over every creeping thing that creeps upon the earth.

God created man in His own image, in the image of God He created him; male and female He created them. And God blessed them, and God said to them, "Be fruitful and multiply, and fill the earth and subdue it; and have power over the fish of the sea and over the birds of the air and over every living thing that moves upon the earth."

And God said, "Behold, I have given you every plant yielding seed which is upon the face of all the earth, and every tree with seed in its fruit; you shall have them for food.

"And to every beast of the earth, and to every bird of the air, and to everything that creeps on the earth, everything that has the breath of life, I have given every green plant for food."

And it was so. And God saw everything that He had made, and behold, it was very good. And there was evening, and there was morning, a sixth day.

Thus the heavens and the earth were finished, and all the host of them. And on the seventh day, God finished His work which He had done, and He rested. So God blessed the seventh day and made it holy. Because on that day, God rested from all His work which He had done in creation.

COMMENT: *This wondrous and sacred creation text is taken from the Holy Bible, Genesis, Chapters One and Two, which is also the First Book of the Hebrew Pentateuch, known as The Five Books of Moses. The Jewish name for Genesis is Bereshith, or* In The Beginning, *which is the first Hebrew word in its opening sentence. The version derives from a text called "P" for Priestly text, said to have been written by several individuals and proclaimed as the Law of God in Jerusalem by the Hebrew Priest, Ezra, 397 B.C. It was expanded and worked on until about 300*

B.C. *Elohim, the Hebrew word for the Creator, is the intensive plural of the word* el *and is always translated as "God." It is used in the above narration with due respect for the Hebrew scribes of the time who used it.*

The Old Testament creation accounts are called Hebrew Myths or the myths of genesis by modern scholars. The Hebrew creation is part of a mon-o-the-is-tic (one god) religious structure. The one-god concept is the main religious form in both Judaism and Christianity. Having one god means having one time and one world in which the heavenly Father is the supreme being. It is creation from the Word. God utters, "Let there be Light," and there was light . . .

MORE ABOUT THESE MYTHS

THE CREATION myths in this book have common features that need some explanation.

Those myths concerned with the creation of earth and beings of earth show the earth still forming. The ground is soft; there are no features such as oceans and mountains. Humans are then created, as in the stories of "The Pea-Pod Man"; "Owner of the Sky"; "An Endless Sea of Mud"; "The Frost Giant"; and "Traveling to Form the World." Other myths tell about a time when the earth and sky were one whole. They were not yet separated, as we see in the myths "Separation of Earth and Sky" and "Marduk, God of Gods."

In the comic myth "Spider Ananse Finds *Something*," heaven, in the beginning, is not separated far enough from earth and so must move higher, out of the way of everyday living. Still other creation myths in this book tell about the cosmic egg, mentioned before, which presents the first of the gods, as in "The Angry Gods" and "Bursting from the Hen's Egg."

There are myths called *Earth-Diver* types in which an animal or other being must dive under water in order to find soil to start the world. This motif can be found in the myths "Turtle Dives to the Bottom of the Sea" and "The Woman Who Fell from the Sky." Examples of still another type, *Creation from the Word,* are "Four Creations to Make Man" and "In the Beginning."

"The Sun-God and the Dragon" and "The Coming of All Things" are examples of the *Creation from Nothing* type of myth. In "Finding Night," Quat and his brothers are born out of a huge stone, Quatgoro—the mother, world-seed. This is a *World-Parent* type of myth, as in "Moon and Sun," in which the Great Mother Nana Buluku creates the world.

It will become obvious that some myths fit more than one type and others defy typecasting. "Bandicoots Come from His Body" and "Sun, Life, Wind, and Death" relate myths that are hard to categorize. In "Bandicoots," sons are born out of the armpit of the god ancestor Karora. In "Sun, Life, Wind, and Death," God Lowa exists, and he creates the Marshall Islands and all creatures of earth. This is a very specific myth expressing how a group of islands came into existence. "Bandicoots," also specific, shows how one clan of the northern Aranda peoples of Australia came to be.

In "First Man Becomes the Devil," God Ulgen creates man, and in many of the stories, man, Erlik, becomes jealous of Ulgen's power. In some versions of the myth, Erlik is depicted as the devil.

Nyambi, of the "Man Copies God" myth, also creates man and lives to regret it.

Two creation stories, "First Man, First Woman" and "In the Beginning," are found in Genesis, Old Testament, in the Holy Bible and in the version of the Holy Scriptures issued by the Jewish Publication Society of America in 1917. They are based on sacred texts written by priestly scholars over several centuries before Christ was born.

The myths, "The Coming of All Things," "The God Brings Fire to Man," and "Pandora" are based on Greek mythology and the evolution of the Greek gods.

USEFUL SOURCES

Arnott, D. *African Myths and Legends Retold*. London: Oxford University Press, 1962.

Beier, Ulli. *The Origin of Life and Death: African Creation Myths*. London: Heineman Educational Books, Ltd., 1966.

Budge, E. A. Wallis. *The Gods of the Egyptians*. Vol. II. London: Oxford University Press, 1904.

Bulfinch, Thomas. *The Age of Fable*. New York: A Mentor Book, NAL, 1962.

———. *The Golden Age of Myth and Legend*. London: Bracken Books, 1985.

Campbell, Joseph. *Myths to Live By*. New York: Bantam Books, 1973.

———. *Oriental Mythology*. New York: Penguin Books, 1976.

———. *Primitive Mythology*. New York: Penguin Books, 1976.

———. *The Hero with a Thousand Faces*. Bollingen Series, Princeton University Press, 1968.

———. *The Masks of God: Occidental Mythology*. New York: Penguin Books, 1976.

Cardinall, A. W. *Tales Told in Togoland*. London: Oxford University Press, 1931.

Christie, Anthony. *Chinese Mythology*. New York: The Hamlyn Publishing Group, Ltd., 1968.

Codrington, R. H. *The Melanesians: Studies in Their Anthropology and Folklore*. London: Oxford University Press, 1891.

Crossley-Holland, Kevin. *The Norse Myths*. New York: Pantheon Books, 1980.

Davenport, William H. *Journal of American Folklore*, "Marshallese Folklore Type." Philadelphia: American Folklore Society, 1953.

Davidson, B. *The African Past*. London: Penguin Books, 1954.

Dixon, Roland B. *Bulletin of the American Museum of Natural History*. Vol. XVIII. Part II, "Maidu Myths."

Doria, Charles, and Lenowitz, Harris. *Origins: Creation Texts from the Ancient Mediterranean*. New York: Anchor Books/Doubleday, 1976.

Edmonson, Muro S., ed. and tr. *The Book of Counsel: The Popol Vuh of the Quiché Maya of Guatemala*. New Orleans, 1971.

Eliade, Mircea. *Gods, Goddesses, and Myths of Creation*. New York: Harper & Row, Publishers, 1974.

Feldman, Susan, ed. *African Myths and Tales*. New York: Dell Publishing Co., 1963.

Ford, D., ed. *African Worlds*. London: Oxford University Press, 1964.

Freund, Philip. *Myths of Creation*. London: W. H. Allen, 1964.

Frobenius, Leo. *The Childhood of Man*. New York: Meridian Books, Inc., 1960.

Goodrich, Norma Lorre. *Ancient Myths*. New York: A Mentor Book, NAL, 1960.

Grant, Michael. *Myths of the Greeks and Romans*. New York: New American Library, 1986.

Grinnel, George Bird. *Blackfoot Lodge Tales*. New York: Charles Scribner's Sons, 1916.

Hale, Horatio. *Journal of American Folklore*, "Huron Folklore." Boston: Houghton Mifflin, for the American Folklore Society, 1888. Reprint Kraus Publishing, New York, 1963.

Hamilton, Edith. *Mythology: Timeless Tales of Gods and Heros*. New York: A Mentor Book, NAL, 1969.

Harper, Robert F. *The God of Hammurabi, King of Babylon*. Chicago: University of Chicago Press, 1904.

Heidel, Alexander. *The Babylonian Genesis*. Chicago: University of Chicago Press, 1951.

Herskovits, Melville J. *Dahomey*. Vol. II. New York: J. J. Augustin, 1958.

Hesiod. *Theogony*. Brown, Norman O., tr. New York: The Liberal Arts Press, 1953.

Holmberg, Uno. *The Mythology of All Races*. Vol. IV, *Siberian Mythology*, "Finno-Ugric." Edited by John A. MacCulloch. New York: Cooper Square Publishers, Inc., 1927.

The Holy Bible, Revised Standard Version. London: Thomas Nelson and Sons, Ltd., 1952.

Leach, Maria. *The Beginning: Creation Myths around the World*. New York: Funk and Wagnalls, 1956.

Leon-Portilla, Miguel, ed. and tr. *Native Mesoamerican Spirituality*. New York: Paulist Press, 1980.

Long, Charles A. *Alpha*. New York: George Braziller, 1963.

Mackensie, D. A. *Myths of China and Japan*. London: 1923.

Nelson, E. W. "The Eskimo about Bering Strait." *18th Annual Report of the Bureau of American Ethnology*. Washington, D.C.: 1899.

Nivedita, Sister, and Coomaraswamy, Ananda K. *Hindus and Buddhists: Myths and Legends*. London: Bracken Books, 1985.

O'Brien, Joan, and Major, Wilfred. *In the Beginning: Creation Myths from Ancient Mesopotamia, Israel, and Greece*. Chicago: The American Academy of Religion, Scholars Press, 1982.

Parrinder, Geoffrey. *African Mythology, Library of the World's Myths and Legends*. New York: Peter Bedrick Books, 1986.

The Pentateuch and Haftorah. 5 vols. Genesis, Exodus, Leviticus. Vol. 5. Hebrew Text, English Translation and Commentary by Dr. J. H. Hertz. London: Oxford University Press, 1929–1936. Based on Jewish Publication Society of America, "American Jewish Version." Philadelphia: 1917.

The Popol Vuh: The Mayan Book of the Dawn of Life and the Glories of Gods and Kings. Dennis Tedlock, tr. New York: A Touchstone Book, Simon & Schuster, Inc., 1986.

The Popol Vuh: The Sacred Book of the Ancient Quiché Maya. English version by D. Goetz and S. Morley from the translation by Adrian Recinos. Norman: University of Oklahoma Press, 1950.

Pritchard, James B., ed. *Ancient Near Eastern Texts relating to the Old Testament*, "Egyptian Mortuary Texts, Myths and Tales." John A. Wilson, tr. Princeton: Princeton University Press, 1950.

Radin, Paul, ed. *African Folktales*. Princeton: Bollingen Series, Princeton University Press, 1952.

Sproul, Barbara C. *Primal Myths: Creating the World*. New York: Harper & Row, Publishers, 1979.

Strehlow, T. G. H. *Aranda Tradition*. Melbourne: Melbourne University Press, 1947.

Verrier, Elwin. *Myths of the North East Frontier of India*. Calcutta: Sree Saraswatty Press, Ltd., 1958.

The pictures in this book were painted
with transparent watercolor on paper handmade
for the Royal Watercolor Society in 1982
by J. Barcham Greene.
Composition by Thompson Type, San Diego, California
in Sabon and Weiss Initials No. 3
Color separations were made by
Heinz Weber, Inc., Los Angeles, California.
Printed by Holyoke Lithograph, Springfield, Massachusetts
Bound by Horowitz/Rae Book Manufacturers, Inc., Fairfield, New Jersey
Production supervision by Warren Wallerstein and Ginger Boyer
Designed by Barry Moser